Sinking Atlantis

Julia Day

GW00707696

Sinking Atlantis

©2000 Julia Day

ISBN 186163 099 9

Internal illustrations and cover painting by Lin Bourne
Cover design by Paul Mason

Published by:

Capall Bann Publishing
Freshfields
Chieveley
Berks
RG20 8TF

Dedication

To my Mother and Father,
without whom I would not be.

and

To all those who have helped on this part of the journey

Introduction

Is it possible to save the planet, reach enlightenment, merge with the Higher Self, write books, run a publishing business, feed the children, water the plants and still have the washing up and dusting completed before the world order changes for ever?

Who needs tidal waves, earthquakes, food scares and genetic changes to worry about when the washing machine is playing up again, the mice are in the chicken bin, the bathroom is full of spiders and your guide refuses to join in the "Meet Your Guide" tapes which you are listening to?

You are told it will all flow as it should when you follow the path of your Highest Good, but no-one bothers to tell you what that is! Or, they all tell you and not only do they disagree, but much of it is downright dangerous and impossible!

Stay calm and still and centred they say. HOW?!

Disclaimer

The author would like to point out that almost everything in this diary is true. That is what makes it unbelievable and so funny.

Any resemblance to persons living or dead is highly likely. The author can only hope that either they cannot recognise themselves or cannot afford a decent solicitor.

 ugust 1998 -
Lughnassadh -
Harvest and
Sacrifice, Death
and Guilt

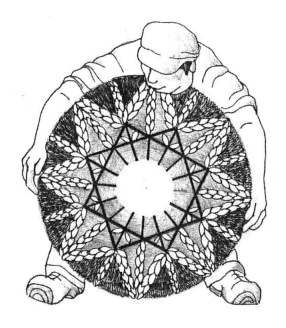

The corn is high and ripening. It waves in the warm breeze like ripples on a pond. Although, nearby, much of it has been cut already and the farmer has sprayed the field with the contents of local septic tanks and cess pits. Another field has been sprayed with the contents of a local piggery. The corn nearest us is not yet cut, which means that the thousands of thunderflies are everywhere, even inside picture frames. I wonder what the farmer plans to spray on the field a few yards from our house?

It is the time of the first harvest, of lammas or loaf mass when farmers would pray for a good harvest to come. In earlier times it was called Lughnassadh after the sun god Lugh.

Lughnassadh according to modern Paganism is the time of the death of the Corn King, the king who sacrifices his life for his people. It is popular to sing John Barleycorn, though which version had best be decided first as I have heard a group give up in confusion as people from different parts of the country each determinedly sang not only different words, but different tunes. All at once.

Traditionally, in the Craft, at Lughnassadh the corn is ripening and the first ears are cut to make a ritual loaf. There is then a celebration which is designed to ensure a good harvest, by no means certain before the days of grain dryers.

Last year Jon and I had the great honour (and guilt?) of killing the Corn King. We cut him down with swords and he was carried off magnificently.

The Corn King was very good looking and acted the part wonderfully, though I was distressed later to hear a rumour that he was gay.

One of our friends years ago lived in a flat on a farm and even though he was American found his electricity bills rather high, even when his flat stood empty for a time. He eventually discovered that not only were the other flats running their freezers off his power, but the farmer was also powering his farmyard, including using the grain dryer!

The bathroom seems to be full of spiders. I have caught them repeatedly and thrown them out of the window. They wait a few seconds and then climb back in again. Jon wonders at first at the sound of me walking repeatedly down the front path and then banging on the gate. Then he realises, yes, I am now walking each one out to the road and banging my long handled spider catcher on the top of the gate to shake them out onto the grass verge. By the fifth I am growing tired. My Hindu, Buddhist and Pagan incarnations are now at war with some obviously less enlightened part of myself which is suppressing a desire to stamp on them. I have considered painting numbers on their backs and taking bets on which one makes it back into the bathroom first.

The garden is full of small creatures carrying on their own little lives and abruptly ending each others'. The blackbird ate the frog and yesterday, the hawk ate a blackbird. I begin to wonder if worrying about being vegetarian or not, (well at least some of the time) is really such an important idea after all. Nothing else seems to feel guilty about what it consumes.

It is a day for contemplation of this human state at this time of increasing closeness to Nature and the momentous Intergalactic energies now pouring towards us.

Should we really be creating a third garden pond, I wonder, when I am told it may be that the coming world changes will result in a 600 foot rise in sea level which will bring the sea right up the Thames valley to somewhere near here? I have wanted to live on the coast for a long time, but now it seems all I have to do is sit still and it will come to me!

Unfortunately, I am not quite sure which side of the coastline we could end up on. Must ask for a new atlas for my birthday. Luckily, we publish a couple of books about boat building.

Enough deep thinking! Time to head for the local Pagan moot at the pub! Luckily, they are one of the few that allow children, so we can go.

At the pub, we are invited to a monthly meeting at someone's house, a caravan weekend in the New Forest and several people put down their names to start a mumming side. We discuss the possibility of getting into Stonehenge for a rite. It is now legal! People do not even stand on your head anymore. Certain folk are most disappointed by this and protest vigorously about being denied the right to be persecuted for their beliefs. It is becoming quite a cool place to be seen! It would be good to go there and perhaps work a rite or just feel the atmosphere without being photographed. Is it really an interstellar gateway? I wonder.

We knew people who lived and worked within the exclusion zone. They had the bad taste, (according to the imported police) to have long hair. Both were apprehended outside their own homes and accused of breaking in and "dossing" on their front lawn. I believe one offered to take the officers inside, using the unusual burglaring tool of a key and show them a photograph of himself inside the house. It was decided by some locals that residents needed identity cards or tee shirts printed with the logo, "I live here". The police would probably have settled for a haircut.

Someone has bought a book and brought it to the pub. People start to read it before they have had a chance to read it themselves. It is a druid's diary no less. It seems to be popular! I hit upon the brilliant idea of writing a diary. (I and about 3,000 other Pagans.) Perhaps I should make it shorter than a year and thus beat the queue when they all start to come out? Or perhaps they will wait until a more suitable time in the year to start their book. I do have a great advantage over most of the opposition though. Few of them run a publishing company.

The same lady gives us some ears of corn from a crop circle that has appeared near Avebury. She and friends arrived there first and had time to hold a quick rite and grab a few ears of corn before an irate farmer appeared. He was left as more Pagans appeared like Indians (sorry, Native Americans) on the sky line looking down at the small circle of wagon-trains, sorry, corn and their guardian hero. Of course, if he had the right sort of access from the road, he could charge £1 entry fee as others have. I am told that they, (crop circles, not farmers) are formed by the Earth releasing energy which naturally comes out in swirling vortices, thus the interesting shapes. Aliens seem to like looking at them too. At least they do not trample the corn, though it is murder getting them to pay an entrance fee.

We go home and put the children to bed.

Then I remember we have forgotten it is Lugnassadh.

Ah well, just time to write this, then off to bed in the early hours of the morning. Enough soul searching for tonight.

8

ugust 6th, Thursday

We have been discussing where to go on holiday. In addition to all the usual questions, can we afford it, who will water the plants and feed the chickens, etc there is also the pressing question of where are we able to travel that is not about to sink?

I rather fancy small flat islands and yet, with giant waves possibly on the increase, this does not seem such a good idea. We like surfing, but there is a limit.

I rather wonder why people who have lived a simple existence, mainly based on coconut trees and local fish, should have their home enveloped by several hundred feet of sea. Or why all the rare creatures should be wiped out. If they are going to be ferried out by UFOs there are going to be an awful lot of sightings.

I think that some of this may well go back to Atlantis. I have never found that the idea of Atlantis quite clicked with me, though we have published several books by authors who do. They describe it in detail and quite differently. I was mentioning this in a talk on Pagan Publishing once. One of our authors, Geoff Hughes, who does believe in Atlantis was present. I talked of the difficult times that so many people face at present and wondered what I had done to deserve it. Suddenly he called out, "It was you! You sank Atlantis!"

Now that must be why I feel guilty all the time. Other people get to be priestesses of Atlantis. Me, I just pulled the plug.

I think he was joking though. Well, I think he was...

Perhaps we should choose a mountain holiday instead? But nowhere near a fault line...

We have decided to leave the choice until later in the year and take our pick from anywhere still above water. Perhaps we should hire a boat?

Until then, we will spend some of our summer on day trips and swimming locally.

# ugust 7th, Friday

Last night the moon was almost full and the sky was clear. I sat looking at it from an open window, nursing Tawny just before I put her to sleep. It would have been nice to sit by our ponds for a while, bathing in the moonlight, but it was midnight before the jobs were done. Perhaps tonight.

For the last two nights a thrumming sound has filled the air as combine harvesters work to the light of the moon. The farmers can go crazy around this time of year, especially if the weather threatens to break. They work all hours and the labourers drive the grain trucks frantically back and forth from the fields. It is best just to keep out of the way. The countryside now is a workplace, not a Disney film set. My Britain's farm animals, (which I still have) never had muddy bottoms. Real cows do.

It may be hard to be a farmer at this time of year, but far worse I think to be a farmer's wife. Can you imagine the tension when the harvester breaks down yet again?

This evening, I went out in the moonlight.

The night air was filled with the sound of the waterfall. Jon has tuned it by the careful placing of pebbles to create the most pleasing flow and musical sound of trickling water. The large pond has many waterlilies almost glowing palely in the moonlight.

The moon seems to be pulsating. I close my eyes and see a magenta centre with an intricate violet web all around it. I open my eyes and then close them again, breathing in the energy. I can see a magenta flame. It burns in a cave at the end of a tunnel, the walls of which are a rich violet purple.

I return indoors and read a book by Terri Hector which may help me to understand the energies that I have been experiencing. It discusses the linking of the physical and spiritual energies of love. If only our experiences in life were as simple and beautiful as fleeting visions suggest. And somewhere a faint whisper comes on the breeze, "But they are....." And if we could see them from that far away, I guess they might be.

# ugust 8th, Saturday

Tonight I went out to meditate with the moon.

I closed my eyes and saw a fruit platter with a grapefruit in the centre, with a spoonful of red fruit in the centre of that and surrounded by large flat edible pieces that I could not identify, but they might have been thin slivers of watermelon.

I search my subconscious to reveal what deep imagery is contained here. Am I consuming the moon energy?

I examine the possibility that I may be hungry. After all, I *am* trying to diet. (Between snacks anyway.)

# August 9th, Sunday

It is 1 o'clock in the morning. I have not been to bed yet. I go outside to look at the moon and then close my eyes.

The moon has become a giant flower, like a sunflower. Its centre is purple and the petals are pale and float out into space. Their edges are formed from a pale golden light.

Tonight, at this time, the moon is reflected in the still water of our pond. I place myself where I can see this reflection and feel the strange, shivery energy which the shimmering image creates in me. It seems to be felt in my stomach area, rather than my head. We often believe that our heads are the only places where realization enters, but energy awareness, enters into our bodies in many places, especially our main energy centres. As our awareness grows, we are taught to feel with different parts of our bodies. Not only do we receive inspiration and psychic knowing, but things may, "grab us by the throat', "enter our hearts", give us a "gut feeling", or even be felt lower down, "turning the bowels to water" as our security is swept away. We must learn again to appreciate these forms of knowing.

There is a massive rustling in the bushes. Two large hedgehogs appear. They bumble across the patio, completely unaware of me. They are hoovering the remains of our outdoor meals, rushing about within three, even two yards of me. Even if I move slightly due to biting midges, they appear blissfully unaware.

One hedgehog rushes to the pond to drink. It swallows for nearly two minutes, (the weather is very hot). I watch the moon's reflection shiver into ten or twenty moons that dance again and again in a rippling line across the surface of the water. At last, the hedgehog has drunk enough and shambles off to find more food. The other has already left.

Wild animals can be quite unaware of people if the people are meditating. I remember leaning back against an oak tree and relaxing. I was brought back to my senses by a terrified squeak. Directly above my head was a terrified squirrel which had almost run over me. It raced back up the tree emitting a series of squeaks very like a manic Sweep, from Sooty and Sweep, but very out of control. I was rather startled too.

Dogs however, seem drawn to meditating forms. One day, I wanted desperately to be alone. This of course, is one of the best ways to draw everything and everybody to you. I went to a wooded area, part of which is now the Newbury By-pass and chose a dark spot at the base of a tree well away from any paths and settled down. (I was in a dark pine mood that day.) A man and his dog appeared and they kept coming. The dog headed for me, the man followed, unaware. At the last minute, I lost my nerve and stood up. It seemed to be that or be run over! They were both startled.

I tried another spot, in the same woods, but further away. I sat on a pine stump. A dog burst through the undergrowth and ran panting at me. "Hello dog", I said and decided to go home. It was then that I found I was lost...

Small children can find you when you are meditating too! And postmen with parcels that they cannot fit through the letter-box. And people who want you to publish their book and think that turning up with it at your house when they have been told definitely not to will endear them and their writing to you.

Also cats, though certain cats are great meditational friends. My dear Grania would come and lie on my chest or at my feet, or sometimes on the bedroom stool and we would ponder the universe together.

Of course, some people might have thought we were just dozing. That is the trouble with really deep meditation. Some people just do not recognise it. I think it is the snoring that may mislead them.

Whilst I typed this, Tawny has been amusing herself with the contents of my office drawers. Amongst other things, dozens of stamps lie on the floor along with business forms which she has helpfully scribbled on and hundreds of previously boxed staples that I should have put elsewhere. I have just run over them with the roller of my office chair, breaking them into even more numerous sharp shards. (I say this for the benefit of all those mums, who wonder how I have time to meditate, write books etc.)

Let me say this much, I am unlikely to be given a Queen's award for housekeeping. To be honest though, it is possible to eat off our floors. Today, before I vacuumed, it was possible to eat Rice Krispies off the kitchen and dining room floors, Bran Flakes off the office floor and peas off the lounge floor.

The spiders are beginning to drive Jon and I mad. I counted seven in the bathroom again. There would have been eight, but one of them was busy eating another. I think his name was Boris. In the Otherworld, he wears tattoos of the names of all the Arachnid girlfriends who have failed to eat him and he rides a motorbike. There are five to ten spiders in nearly every room. The "an it harm none" rule is stretching and Jon, (who has also been removing them) is beginning to consider vacuuming them up.

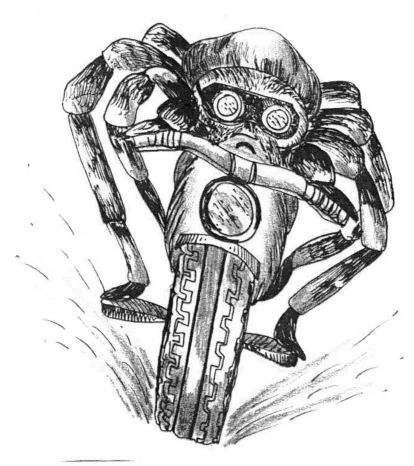

The porch is also full of ants, who try to swarm every few days. They ran over the kitchen for weeks as I tried to apply mind power, (as suggested by Betty Shine) to get them to move out. My previous year's attempts of placing water and sweet substances outside for them seem to have failed. Instead. I have the horrible impression that the word, "snack-bar" is written large on our home in insect language.

It seems to be a time of death. One of our chickens died this week. We bought four rescued ex-battery hens to add to our ancient bantams. The cockerel was delighted, but the hens promptly tried to murder the bantams, so they are in separate runs. When one of the new hens became ill, the cockerel was very unkind to her. Animals can be very cruel. It seems they have a disease which is prevalent at the moment which makes the eggs very thin shelled. The lady I bought them from says it is a form of air-borne bronchitis.

I wonder if something is affecting the wild birds too as we have found several lying dead recently. One died in our wildlife pond, fouling the water. It was necessary to pump out much of the polluted water and unavoidable to therefore kill much of the wildlife in it. One begins to feel that Nature is conspiring to press the inevitability of death upon us.

Even our male Siamese fighting fish is ailing. If you have ever thought of keeping a few fish, consider strongly whether or not to start with an aquarium. Believe me, they are hard work. We recently bought a male Siamese fighting fish. The man in the shop said he would mix with our angel fish in the big tank. We put him in. He was terrified. If we put him in our small tank, would he eat the baby fish? No, said the man in the shop. He did. I caught the last survivor as he was eying it up for size. If he had a female would he be happier? Would he go in the big tank then? Yes, said the man, but we must buy more than one female. We bought them. They went into the big tank and they all hid. He was not interested in them. The man in the shop suggested he was gay.

We put them back in the small tank. They ate the next hatching of babies. Then a female died. Now the male is ill. I have bought them special food and tested and changed the water. It has cost quite a bit of money and I have spent hours worrying about them. Tara, our daughter, aged nearly seven, is sad about her baby fish. I am reaching exasperation point here. The man in the shop has cheerfully made lots of money. I am becoming suspicious.

18

The corn hare, (well rabbit) has also become deeply involved in this time of death and sacrifice. About as deeply involved as it is possible to be, really. It is dead. Tho wild rabbit entered our garden and Jon followed after it with his air rifle, having seen what rabbits can do to vegetable patches. Tara ran around indoors with her toy gun, torn between loyalty to the hunter and to the cute fluffy bunny. That particular hunting trip was unsuccessful and the moral dilemma was solved for us, as Jon had said he thought it would be. A few days later, the rabbit was hit and killed by a car. Sacrifice accomplished.

It was sad to relate that if Jon had shot it, the logical thing to do, in order not to waste it, was to eat it and yet neither Jon nor I felt that we could skin and gut it. In the same way, we have given away our extra cockerels, when it would be sensible to eat them ourselves. They have had a happy and healthy life. It is not possible to keep them all for it is cruel to the hens to have too many, quite apart from space, money and noise and they would taste better than any meat we could ever buy. Yet we give them away. I knew one mostly vegetarian lady who would eat her own cockerels, but then her husband carried out the gruesome parts.

Much as it is explained to me that all life is but spirit and these creatures all go to their spirit counterpart to be born again, (assuming we have not committed the unbelievable crime of making them extinct), I still find myself mourning them. I find it no small thing when an animal with whom I have shared an awareness of the world changes from a companion to an empty shell, a piece of meat or rubbish which must be disposed of before it decomposes. Perhaps I should have fewer animals.

I have come a long way from sorrow at each passed road kill. Still, it seems that in our development we may at first care nothing for other creatures and then we may learn respect. Then, we reach a stage where perhaps we disadvantage ourselves to massive degrees in order not to harm them. Eventually we may find that to live on this Earth without harming anything is an impossibility. "And it harm none" is a nice idea which simply cannot work on the physical plane.

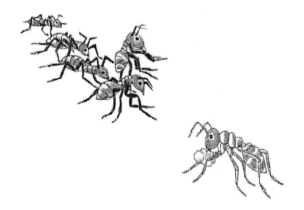

# August 13th, Thursday

Jon vacuumed the spiders.

Within 2 days there were eight back in the bathroom.

There are a group of them lurking in a gang at the top of the stairs and more in our bedroom. Fruit flies swarm above the fruit bowls and ants wander about the house. I read that the better class of astral plains do not contain insects as they are a very low form of life and stay nearer to the planet. I wish this lot would buzz off!

The tension is mounting over the cutting of the corn. The farmer always seems to leave the field near us to the very last. The weather threatens to break and the tension mounts. Will he wait until it rains again this year? The insect problems grow worse and worse until he cuts it.

The heat ripples off the corn. This brings another swarm, this time of gliders. The hot air above the corn rises in a swirling thermal and lifts them into the air. As our fields are amongst the last, the gliders congregate in a flowing, escalating flock. At least they are quiet.

The Siamese fighting fish died. We took the last female back to the shop and asked for our money back. I would have been fine in my resolve to buy no more fish, had the man given me cash, but he only offered credit. So we bought three more platys. We asked for a male and two females. (You are meant to keep more females.) The man flipped the last fish into the bag quickly and walked off rapidly. They were all bagged up before I could reach the counter with Tara crying, "That was not the one I wanted!" Sure enough, when we reached home, there were two males. I am doing something wrong here, aren't I? Anyway, they all seem happy today.

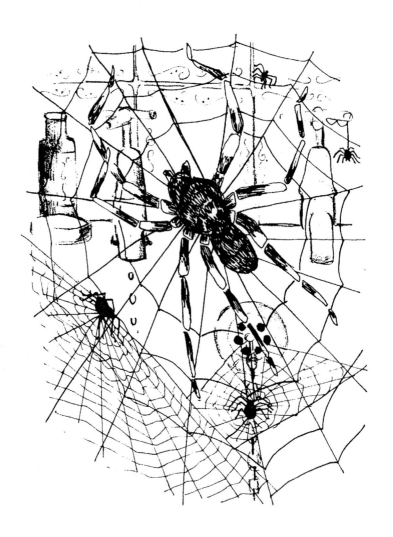

# August 17th, Monday

On Friday 14th the farmer finally started to cut the corn in the near field. The cloud of chaff billowed all around the machine so that it appeared to be on fire.

That night, it rained.

Luckily, the weather improved for the weekend, so we have spent the last three days out. This is just as well, as our new neighbours, who moved in commenting on how nice and quiet it is around here, have not only taken to playing a drum kit, sometimes at 1 o'clock in the morning, but on Saturday were playing music for all the surrounding people to share. Many people cannot stand the country. With luck, they may move out soon.

On Friday we went to Oxford as part of my desperate attempt to find something new to wear to a family christening that does not look like a potato sack. No such luck! Shop after shop was filled with the most ghastly, woman-hating rags I have ever seen. They make women flat-chested who have full busts and they create extra lumpy hips, stomachs and bottoms in a monstrous way. If I were to start fashion lines based on such styles, I would call them, "The Misogynist" and "Le Frump".

People wandered the streets in the sales without buying anything. Jon noticed that hardly any full carrier bags. Marks and Spencers contained rack after rack of what seemed to be thousands and thousands of what I perceived to be baggy, saggy, lumpy misfitting dresses, knocked down in price. They still did not seem to be selling. One American lady commented to me on the price of British clothes also. They are far cheaper in America. "What do British women find to wear?"

The city toilets were despicable. I will not describe them. When one thinks that Oxford is also where many foreigners visit and gain an impression of this country, they cannot have too good an impression. I may be just a country mouse, but there seems to be something increasingly wrong in our cities. A short while ago, I walked with the children down the Tottenham Court Road in London. A youth in a group with his friends collided with six year old Tara, knocking her to the ground. He let out a string of foul abuse and slouched on. It seemed some kind of hell.

On Saturday we went swimming. Following a terrible accident last time we went, I left Tawny's nappy on as she played by the side of the pool. It grew bigger and bigger as the gel soaked up more and more of the pool. Eventually, it burst, filling the area with lumps of swollen gel. Why is nothing ever simple? The only good bit was that it was my turn to swim. Jon had to deal with it.

On Sunday, just after getting up, I was suddenly struck by an inspired idea about original sin. It was not eating apples, disobeying God or having sex, it was guilt. It is guilt that causes so much trouble. The human race has had people making it feel guilty ever since. Man has blamed woman and the church blamed man and woman. Centuries of guilt manipulation, over an apple for goodness sake! All Adam and Eve had to do was say, "Sorry if it upset you, but we ate the fruit". I mean, what is free will for?

Later on Sunday we went to the Cotswold Wildlife Park and ate one of Jon's brilliant picnics. This place is not greatly known as a sacred site but it is one of those many other places where one can find an all pervading peace. It even seems to survive despite the sometimes dreadful people who may visit. The wild animals, such as small birds, are tame too.

There is a wonderful, huge, gnarled old tree near the cafe. We just had to take photographs! No, sorry we did not link hands and hold a rite amongst the icecream eating visitors. But I know Pagans who would have... Probably naked...

There were all manner of rare animals there, rare rhinos, zebras, big cats, even a recently born tapir, but Tawny seemed to like the ducks best. I asked Tara which she liked best. She said the ducks too. She also liked the "wobblies", (wallabies).

In the children's zoo, I took photographs of the children and goats who always seemed to turn the wrong way at the last second. As I took one, the goat jumped sideways, Tara jumped backwards in fright, Tawny fell over and at the same moment a stray gust of wind blew my hat off. I think I may just have a good shot of my foot! (In fact it was my belt pouch!)

Zoos, (sorry, wildlife parks) are of course, supermarkets for shamans. Jon managed to reach a crane feather out of a run by using a twig. Last time he gained a beautiful black crane feather, though we had to ask the keeper for help with that. Yesterday we saw a boy walking past with a magnificent black and white crane feather, quite huge. We considered mugging him, but he was with his family, so we thought better of it.

I found a blackbird feather.

That night, there was a baby hedgehog in our car port. Everyone rushed out to see it.

Today, I have not been meditating, having spiritual awakenings or holding Inter Galactic healing rites in the garden. I have been trying to retrieve the house from the results of three days out in a row during the summer holidays with the children home.

One day an author will phone up to ask if we have read their manuscript yet, set it yet, or organized life size cardboard cut outs of them, looking like Jilly Cooper or Terry Pratchett, to be placed in all major shops, but especially ones near them where there friends and their Mum can see them, and when we reply, wonder what hit them. I think I rather shocked one author some time ago when I said "Tough" to them. Twice. Certain days, it is more likely to be, "Aaaargghh!"

Today, Jon phoned to ask me to order a new cheque book as our trigger cheques, (the ones that they use to decide when to post you a new cheque book) had been posted to America and Australia and were therefore going to take a long time to arrive. Realising how fast the cheques are going out at present, I phoned the building society. Could I have two cheque books please? No, I could not. Well, in that case, I would like to order another cheque book and then another one straight after that. The lady agreed. I could hear her nearly laughing on the phone. That it seems, would be alright. The world does work in a funny way!

Years ago, I needed one foot, (no metric here!) of carpet tape to mend my boot. The lady told me that they could only sell it in fractions of a yard. In that case, could I have one third of a yard please?

There was a pause. Eventually, she agreed to sell me one half or one quarter!

And we find the ideas of fairies or aliens strange!

Oh yes, and clothes that I had ordered from a catalogue arrived today. They fitted. They had shape and style. One of them poured on. It can be done!

We are currently trying to decide between two distributors who each want an exclusive deal, that is, to be the only distributors in their part of the world. Without telling me what he had planned, Jon told me to shut my eyes. He put a piece of paper in my hand. "How does that feel?

"Light, with energy rising off it." He swapped it for another piece of paper.

"And that?"

"Heavy. Very heavy. But then it is much heavier paper. It is pushing my hand to the floor." They were both identical sheets of fax paper. They came from the two different distributors. If he had told me what he planned, my conscious mind would probably have cut in and blocked what I was feeling. As it is, we have something to help us make our decision. (Eventually we went with a third distributor who was 'just right'!)

You see, energy stays with the written word. If it is printed in a book or even sent around the world by fax, the energy is there. If you read a book, it is more than the words that will uplift you, heal you, or drag you down, drain you or make you shake with laughter. It is the energy that the author has expressed into the writing.

That should make you think!

# August 20th, Thursday

Yesterday we went shopping. We drove home with the car window wound down. To our great surprise and that of the bird, a pigeon flew in through the open window of our car and settled, wings outspread upon the shopping. Jon turned the car into our driveway and opened his door. The pigeon flew off, leaving two feathers to add to my blackbird feather.

As we ate out on the patio later, a baby pigeon landed on the barbecue, (which was not lit). "You've got the right idea mate" says Jon, "Wait there while I get some charcoal". Somehow, I just cannot see Jon making it to being vegan.

It reminded me of a pigeon that I saw a few years ago with a broken wing. I was torn between my desire to help and the fact that since they are great destroyers of crops, helping it was not uppermost on Jon's mind. He said something about redcurrant jelly, if I remember right. Sometimes, though, an animal looks at you and that look can stay with you all your life. There are accounts of people becoming vegetarian after one look from an animal they killed.

It is strange, but when I have a very unusual animal encounter, it rarely seems to be with the magical animals that are included in all the books. "You see an eagle flying by, (turn to page 26) and then later, pass a dolphin, (page 15)" and so on. Mine are either very ordinary or wildly unlikely.

I did have a rather strange session with birds once. There was a white budgie and a white small cockatoo type bird and a

28

small grey parrot which arrived in our garden. I believe they must have escaped from an aviary. When I phoned someone to ask for spiritual advice on what was happening, (perhaps I should have phoned someone more practical, but could not think who,) they also had met a white budgie flying free. They had caught theirs, which is more than I could. I had also recently met a swan which landed on the road by our house. They also had rescued a swan from a road. There were other similarities with experiences. I seemed to have phoned just the right person.

It seems that birds and feathers can symbolise messages from the world of spirit. White birds can symbolise passing an initiation.

Other birds have also been omens for me. A pair of rooks showed me to beware of other's greed and envy as three other pairs of rooks stole the twigs from their nest as they turned their back from making it. They built very high in a tree near our house, not normally built in. The three human couples duly showed themselves throughout the year. I knew at the time it was a sign, though I was grieved to find out who the people were that I had been warned about.

The farmer is back cutting his corn. He is using the oldest machine that I have ever seen, I think, barring ancient collections at shows and old photographs. It does not actually have a man holding a pitchfork stood on top, but seems to be not too many grades up. I presume that his machine really did break down with a vengeance this year. It is a very big field and a small machine and so is taking a long time to cut. He also has to reverse back and go over some of the field again. The chaff blows everywhere. We are about one hundred feet from the field and I just managed to shut the upstairs window in time as a rolling cloud of dust boiled over the neighbour's garden. No washing out today.

I brought the dry washing in last night to keep it safe as Jon was using a hosepipe and then a water battle developed between him and Tara. I put the dry washing in the hall. Unfortunately, Tara came indoors and fell over, spilling water over it. They decided to rehang the now wet washing in the carport. Unfortunately, they did not notice dropping some of it into a mixture of mud, sawdust and cement. Today, I have left the washing safely in the machine. It may be wet, but at least it has been clean all day.

I have discovered at last why I have problems with house-work - I lack servants!

I watched a hare running over the stubble the other day. Animals become frightened and confused. A rabbit ran onto the road yesterday and then sat there, forcing us to stop our car. Then it ran back. It did not seem to have mixi, just be confused.

My Uncle Victor was the son of an estate foreman and carpenter on Earl Nelson's estate. He has a piece of timber from "The Victory". Years ago, as the last sheaves in the centre of the field were cut, all the animals that had fled there would run out, making a meal for the agile and quite a sport too. The gypsies that had worked on the harvest would throw their sticks and try to hit a rabbit. He tried and succeeded. The gypsies were impressed. Years later, now a policeman, passing a rabbit warren, he tried the same trick with his truncheon. He missed. He eventually decided to follow the path that his truncheon had cut through the dew and found the stick. He was very late back to the station, as it took him ages to find the truncheon and of course, he could not tell them why.

Pigeon

Pigeon with a broken wing,
You speak to me
With your soft sad eye,
Soul to soul.

The vet would suggest
An injection
Leading to infinity.

Being practical,
You eat our peas,
Pigeon people.

The gardener has a gun.
He does not plan to write you a poem,
Only an epitaph.

You have disappeared.
Into the etheric?
I do not know.
You leave me with a sad eye
And a distaste for death.

 ugust 21st, Friday

On our television screens, we continue to see the results of the bomb blast which destroyed and forever changed so many lives a few days ago in Omagh.

What can possibly be the sense of such a senseless act?

And yet there is a sense. Not only were the dead not "just" men, but women and children, but also they represented all the different areas of the troubles in Ireland, Protestant, Catholic, Northern and Southern. (And would the South of Ireland really want to become one with people who commit such acts?) Was it "alright" when they did it to each other or to us?

There is a time when so much darkness and hatred has accumulated that it can only be released in acts of horror and violence.

Everyone could feel that they had lost someone who was somehow part of "their own" group. Until Protestant weeps for dead Catholic and Catholic weeps for dead Protestant, the troubles will continue. The energy created by hate and fear is massive and a few people have benefited in crime and violence for a long time. Until people learn to combat the energy of fear, hatred and evil with that of the strength of love, the problems cannot be beaten.

Love is not a soft and soppy thing here. It is love like a sword, honed in suffering. The people must love and have confidence enough in themselves to stop it and the determination that such atrocities are not allowed to continue in the name of either politics or religion. Ideas of peace and love are terrifying to those who carry out the acts of terrorism. They will be like bugs crawling from the light, trying to destroy what they can. When people respond with compassion, what can they do but other evil acts, increasingly showing themselves as the warped individuals that they are, losing support all around.

There are those who have lost their loved ones who again and again have called for peace rather than vengeance. Maybe this time, enough people will listen to turn the energies around.

The Americans too are shocked by yet another bomb blast affecting themselves. Yet they collect money to support the Irish bombs. They too have a lot of painful understanding about to be brought home.

 ugust 25th,
Tuesday

We went swimming at a different pool this weekend, one we had not visited before. Tawny wore waterproof pants. There were no difficult incidents.

It was a leisure pool with waves and bubbles and a flume which is a massive enclosed water slide about three times the length of the pool which snakes backwards and forwards as it descends from the ceiling.

Tawny loved the shallow water with bubbles and it helped her overcome her fear of water, which she gained when she fell in the garden pool some weeks ago. She had floated face down in the fishpond with her arms out-stretched. I lifted her out in seconds but the incident has stayed with both of us. At least in the shallow water, she played and enjoyed herself.

The waves were great fun! I thought there was a five minute warning and was nearly caught in the roped off area unawares as they started. My mother was swimming in a wave pool unaware that such things existed when the wave machine was set in motion right next to her. It was quite a surprise for her!

The flume took a certain amount of courage on my part, combining height and enclosure. I went down it once. It seems it is sound proofed as else, I am sure my screams would have been heard in the next county! Tara had several turns. It was mostly children that have the nerve to ride it.

This week we aim to return when Tawny is at nursery, so Jon, Tara and I can all join in all the time and plan to go for the session where the waves are at their highest.

Tara made a friend there and we were memorising phone numbers so that they could phone each other. Remembering tips given by those who have incredible memories, I used images, seven dwarves, six geese a laying and so on. I must try to learn other numbers in the same way as that little girl's phone number now seems engraved on my long term memory better than my own.

Two years ago, neither Jon nor Tara could swim and both overcame their fear of water and now we all go frequently to swim. It is wonderful exercise as well as fun and great for relaxing. I do wish that those who swim to release anger would be a little more careful though. In our more usual pool, some of the men would thrash up and down, choosing to swim in the slower roped off lane and crashing painfully into the women in a manner that suggested they were doing it on purpose. It is rare that I feel like smashing my elbow hard into someone else, but with one man, it came close. Having collided with Jon, who is somewhat harder, he thought better of it after that.

Today I took the children to the park. Three more children came in, a boy about seven and two toddlers. There was no adult there at first. The youngest toddler caught her fingers in the gate and lost her shoe and the second climbed the larger climbing frame and slipped between the bars. She was trapped, hanging, folded between the bars, screaming. I ran across the play ground and supported her, pulling her out. Tara helped the youngest to put her shoe on. Eventually a woman arrived. She seemed quite unworried and did not hurry even when she must have seen me rush to help the child. I felt that she was "looking after them" for someone else.

Several years ago I found a small toddler stood all alone beside rushing water, stood on the very edge where it poured out of a large pond to squeeze under a bridge. No other person was in sight. Luckily, I guessed correctly where the child had come from and returned him to his mother who was just running out of her door with a worried look on her face. Who knows, had I been a minute later...?

When I was small, I did something similar to my mother, wandering out into the road one night. She answered the door to a strange man saying. "Excuse me Madam, is this your baby?"

It becomes even more confusing when we are told that all things are not co-incidence. So what do we change? As they say, it seems wise to keep your powder dry and tie your camel however much you trust the Divine. Especially with small children.

I think there must be many guardian angels of small children and they are probably very tired angels too by the time a few such adventures have passed.

August 26th, Wednesday

The farmer finally sprayed the field with manure. We cannot decide whether it is pig or human, but the effect is much the same.

Today the weather seems to have turned very cold, not so much an Indian summer, as a Siberian one. The temperatures in Scotland have fallen to 4 degrees centigrade at night recently and I have both duvets back on the bed. What do the inhabitants of other countries ever find to talk about when they do not have our weather?

Having so enjoyed playing with the water at the pool, Tawny continues in our bathroom. This week, she has poured pints if not gallons of water onto the bathroom floor, which at the moment has carpet tiles. (Very wet carpet tiles.) At least it is downstairs, so the water is draining through the floorboards to underneath the house.

I heard of a plumber who had great trouble explaining to a customer why he could not fit a sunken bath tub into her upstairs bathroom, not unless she wanted a very unusual feature in her dining room ceiling.

The bathmat has gone slimy and mouldy and is hanging in disgrace on the line. It is also coming apart, so I think I will be brave and throw it in the bin. It always makes me feel guilty to throw anything away. When my brother helped me move into my first house he said, "I have never seen so many boxes full of things that no-one could ever possibly want."

Sometimes I imagine the team from "Changing Rooms" coming to decorate the bathroom, but I just know that the pine door, cupboard and shelves would be too much for them and they would have to paint them magenta pink and nail sheets of aluminium to them, whilst painting the bath with a colour which starts to peel off the second they have stopped filming. Then they would paint the floor with something that will never dry.

None of the neighbours would trust me back anyway, not since we painted the dining room orange. I thought it would come out terracotta, though I suppose the words, "Etruscan Orange" on the tin were a slight clue. We sponged it over with apricot anyway and it was quite fun. We all sponged different parts of the room, including Tara so the pattern changes as you look at different parts of it, but at least Tara does not say it makes her feel sick anymore.

We allowed Tara to choose the colours for her bedroom at about the same time. That was when we discovered her slight blue/green colour blindness. Yes, I know it is usually red/green. I have it too and it took me years to realise it. Jon used to work with a man who was red/green colour blind. He used to wire plugs and had to ask which wire was which. It could have been worse - he might have worked for bomb disposal! Once they made a bad mistake and let him choose carpet tiles for the office. They were a completely different colour to what he thought and unusable.

I am trying to work up to having the bathroom floor covered in a waterproof surface. It would make sense in the kitchen too, though, since we wonder if we should extend that one day, it would feel wasteful.

The house seems too small. Having two children and a business running partly from home, takes up space alarmingly. I dread to think how long it would take me to count all the books in the house, for instance, let alone consider how many there are and that is bearing in mind that our publishing stock is held at the office up the road. I have heard that a house contains on average only twelve books. Well we have streets full here.

Somehow everything seems to be mixed up. My office contains Tawny's clothes and the nappy bin. Jon's study has a push-chair. Tawny's bedroom contains a filing cabinet and so on.

I am one of those people who believes that my life should be all ordered simplicity and the truth of it is nothing like it. I read catalogues and believe that all those strange shaped "organizers" will really change my life. Eventually, if I bought them all, I would probably need an organizer to keep them in.

Things just seem to cause more work, need greater storage and organising and again and again fail to create the great sense of achievement, organization, sense of being loved and fulfilled and everything else that is promised. What they do seem to do is take up space and break down.

The aquariums are a case in point as I try to keep all the little fish alive and happy. The pump for Tara's aquarium broke the other night and I was dismantling and cleaning the engine after midnight. I was not even sure I could do it, but the fish needed it. As it was, most of the fish became ill afterwards and I had to treat them with medicine. We now have five new platy babies. Tara is delighted, but they look set to overfill the tank, leaving no room for the little neons that I wanted in the first place. Life seems to keep forming these paradoxes.

Now, the washing machine will not spin properly. Jon kindly hung the washing out for me and I realised in the early evening that it is still soaking wet. We paid for an expensive guarantee. If there is a problem, it is not easy to find the correct phone numbers, certificates and so on. When I do, there may be a long wait trying to get through on the phone. Eventually, I am told a man will turn up some time during the day, maybe next week.

When he came last time, he wanted to try out the machine with a load of washing in. Jon was kindly helping him. What happened next is a man thing. Only men would do it. They ignored the great mound of dirty washing that had piled up during the several days waiting for him to come and went to the airing cupboard. They loaded all my clean, dry, aired large towels into the machine. After watching them for a while, the man said he could not find the fault and went away. I was left with all the dirty washing and a machine load of towels. I could not be angry with Jon, because he had stayed back from work in order to wait for the man and anyway, it is something to do with the male genes.

It was of course raining. And the machine is obviously, still faulty. Should I now steel myself to phone them again?

I bought a book on assertiveness recently. I could not see that it helped me at all. I decided that if anyone gave me trouble, I would hit them with the book.

I wanted to go on a course about assertiveness years ago when I was a teacher. Unfortunately, I had to get permission from my headmaster, a very unhelpful person. I did not go on the course. I did not have the nerve to ask him. I felt that it was probably full, as are all such courses, of Boudiccas and women wearing dungarees with spanners through their noses.

And like many ex-teachers, I still have nightmares...

A lady I knew was considering whether to go on a course about decision making, but she just could not decide....

 eptember 1st, Tuesday

I am currently reading a book in which the author claims to have been operated on by extra terrestrials. He had operations which can be verified by X-rays and yet these operations were not carried out by the normal hospital system and could not normally have been successful with the technology of the time. He remembers being operated on by extra-terrestrials in a space ship.

Jon woke up on Saturday with a three inch scar across his chest. He could not remember where he had received such a wound. Spooky! (or Spocky).

We have been swimming twice more, but decided not to go to the "Wet and Wacky" session again, especially after three adolescents on a raft landed on top of me in the shallow area and pinned me to the ground during the wave session, grazing my knee and denting my pride. Several dozen children had arrived from a holiday club and it all became too frantic. The next session was calmer. I had another go on the water slide and this time kept my eyes open and my mouth shut. Our holiday at home seems to be working quite well.

The bathroom is full of spiders again. Jon had another vacuuming session and we have both been carrying them outside, but they keep appearing. I threw out a 'tarantula', all by myself. I managed to catch it in my long-handled spider scoop.

On Sunday we went to the Christening of my brother's twin children. Outside the church a lady announced in a voice that carried right down the road that she was wearing the outfit that she wore to Buckingham Palace. Just inside the church, she said, in a voice that rang off the rafters, "This gives me another chance to wear the outfit that I wore to Buckingham Palace". Luckily the stained glass windows survived. Just inside the door of my Mother's house she announced that she was wearing the outfit that she wore to Buckingham Palace. "I am name dropping aren't I" she added.

In my Mother's lounge, on top of the television, sat the photographs of my brother, at Buckingham Palace, receiving his MBE. Regarding sibling rivalry, I am not sure that I can beat that one. Game to us though I think.

The service was conducted by the retired vicar from the village, now in his eighties. He remembered me as a child, "Always asking questions". It was a shame that we did not have more time to talk. Mind you, I am not quite sure that I would have had the nerve to tell him the interesting theory that during my last life I was a nun. As he said to me twenty years ago, "It never quite clicked with you Julia". Too much of it last time round! He added his own personal touches to the service, shouting "Hurray!" and "Voila!" at times.

Afterwards, my Grandmother, in her nineties described to me how she was recently interviewed to collect information about life in the Mendips earlier this century. She showed them her Morris dancing medal. It seems that local modern, male teams had declared that only men had danced Morris in the Mendip hills. Despite poor eyesight and not being quite as sprightly on her feet as she was a year or so ago, she made her way across Bristol to an event where Morris teams were gathered in a restaurant. She rounded on them firmly, not only telling them that women had danced Morris, but showing them the medal and photographs to prove it! My Mum was

Top: My grandfather, Thomas Hancock, back row on the left.
Bottom: My grandmother Gwendoline Lyons is front left.

terribly embarrassed when she heard what had happened. "They don't dance Morris properly now," my grandmother said to me, "They only do it for fun."

Tara played the drum for a Morris team recently and she played well enough at six years old for them to let her play whilst they danced.

I nearly followed in the family footsteps at college, learning Morris dancing, but the ladies' team, although learning all the dances well, could never decide what to wear.

# eptember 3rd, Thursday

At last! it is the end of the school holidays. Today, Tara went back to school and Tawny is at nursery. Unfortunately, I spent most of the day feeling ill.

We spent the last day of the holiday visiting Longleat. We passed Cley Hill near Warminster on the way. It used to be known for UFO sightings. We did not see any, but then it was cloudy.

In the safari park, I stroked a camel, until a member of staff asked me not to. A tiger came right up to the car which was wonderful. The wolves however, were sleeping. We sat in the car looking at the distant patches of fur muttering, "One twitched an ear" or "One moved a paw". It said in the guide book that we might hear them howl, "More like snoring" said a disappointed Jon who really likes wolves. We went into another couple of shaman's supermarkets with African masks and drums in one. Tawny escaped from her buggy and I was busy replacing toys on the shelves when she disappeared from the shop. A lady pointed her out to me. She had run out of the shop clutching six cuddly animals.

As we drove home, the skies went the strangest beige colour and the rain poured down. Jon muttered about "Ragnarok".

Today I have been reading information that Rik Dent had copied off the Internet for us. It consisted of a great deal of material about Aspartame and how bad it is for us.

It is claimed that studies have repeatedly stated in America that it should be banned but oddly, such advice is never followed. We discovered how many things it is in, including vitamin tablets and other health products, which I take every day. Following other material which he copied off the Internet, I have been reducing my intake of refined carbohydrates. Unfortunately, I now seem to be suffering attacks of sickness and feeling faint and dizzy linked to low blood sugar. This it seems is a sign that I had a problem and need to avoid the refined carbohydrates. The only answer seems to be to keep eating other things!

I remember trying a chocolate diet once. It was most enjoyable. The only drawback was that I gained half a stone in weight in just two weeks.

The feeling that we are being fed "food" which is not food and may be bad for us grows day by day. The British scientist who stated that genetically engineered potatoes were bad for rats was sacked recently. He is perhaps lucky. In America, he would probably have had a fatal car accident.

It is amazing that at the time I am writing this, we do not have to be informed on packaging that food is genetically engineered, for the simple reason that we would no doubt prefer not to eat it. The buds of the genetically engineered cotton have dropped off and farmers want to sue Monsanto. Genetically engineered crops turn up miles away from where they are planted.

In America, a group is trying to push through legislation that will make the term "organic" quite meaningless and make it law that no other definition than their own may be used. This means something good in fact. It means that those who make money from practises that we may not agree with or benefit from are scared and on the run.

Even Vegans who until recently may have felt smug as Salmonella and BSE run riot are now not too sure. The genetically engineered soya beans from America were mixed with those which are not and they are in everything apart from organic products.

One of our authors, Chris Thomas, believes that genetic engineering was the reason that Atlantis had to be totally destroyed. That is why we so rightly fear it.

It is also true that natural things all have a particular harmony. Is that present in these strangely modified crops?

And whilst we mention strange changes, the incidence of floods which then do not return to normal quickly are increasing. Jon notices that even foreigners are beginning to discuss the weather, those from Texas especially, with first droughts there and now floods. As the weather changes, El Nino should have its own television series soon.

September 10th, Thursday

I blame "Changing Rooms' myself. One third of our bedroom, which was a very neutral cream, cream walls, cream bedding, cream curtains and with plain pine furniture, is now a violent cerise plum.

The colour was my fault. I chose it. I thought it would be a dusky plum shade, but that is not what has happened. Jon disappeared upstairs with a sponge and the paint. When I went upstairs and saw it for the first time, I screamed. I suppose this was not very tactful. The light, spaced out dabbing of faint colour I had envisaged had turned into strong, closely placed patches of deep, vibrant, well, cerise plum is the nearest I can get.

It is not even one wall, but uncompleted parts of different surfaces and now that Jon has lost his nerve, (I suppose I should not have screamed, or laughed hysterically) now looks to remain in this strange half altered state. It is rather like the moon-change of a werewolf frozen in mid-transformation.

I decided, after this "holiday" that I needed help with the house. I simply cannot write and work for the company and care for the children and the animals and plants and do the housework. Unfortunately, several other mums all came to the same conclusion and the Post Office window is full of cards all asking for help in the home. In an area which officially has zero unemployment at present, it is tricky to find help with all those little jobs.

I have always felt dust to be most unfair. I leave it alone. Why doesn't it leave me alone? Housework must be one of the most thankless tasks in the Universe, like filling in the hole you have just dug a million times over.

Tawny continues flooding the bathroom. I now remove the carpet tiles before a bath. She is also soaking the kitchen floor. I think they will have to be refloored with a waterproof surface. Last time we had new flooring, the men threw the old carpet out on top of my plant pots, around the front door, thus wrecking a plant, rushed off with the original flooring that I had said I wanted to keep and left razor blades all over the house, even in rooms they had not been fitting, including our toddler's bedroom. I do not seem to have much luck with workmen. Like that old song, "It was on a Monday morning when the gasman came to call...." they chip ceilings, permanently ruin carpets, get tar on the settee and pour filthy water down through the airing cupboard which was of course, totally full of clean linen, bedding, towels and dried washing.

Though I guess I do not have too much to worry about, when I see pictures of Bangladesh, flooded for weeks.

I went to see the homeopath yesterday. I went into the blue room, which is a restful peach with restful deep blue carpets, curtains, furniture and gloss work. I wanted to copy the room in our dining room and kitchen, but it turned out orange and we still have the same cream curtains and brown carpet, so it was not the same. We painted the doors deep blue though. One started chipping straight away.

My homeopath offers a range of alternative treatments. One is a Bicom machine. This feeds back a kind of cleansed energy to the person using it. You hold brass balls in your hand, or sometimes put your hands and feet on brass plates. When I first used it, he said I would feel nothing. But I could feel a strong energy rising up my legs from the brass plates under my feet. "Are you sure I will feel nothing?" "Yes", "Because if it gets much stronger, I will have to do something."

The energy was very like Earth energy rising up the legs, especially at a very strong site like Avebury. Also, I could feel the energy begin in my hands. He said that only one in twenty people would feel anything. I described where the energy entered and what it was doing in my body. There was a sensation of balancing around my pelvis. It seems that very few people are that sensitive to the energy.

It would be wonderful to relax and just experience all this, but I am accompanied by my toddler, Tawny. So whilst this goes on, I am passing sticklebricks to her with my feet and pulling funny faces to amuse her. "Oh dear" she sighs as the big tub of bricks falls over and makes a terrible mess on the floor.

Meditation is much the same if she is around. Have you ever tried to meditate with a small child bouncing on your stomach? "Find a space and time when you will not be disturbed" the tapes say. Ha! Enlightenment it seems, is not for those with small children. We just get exhausted instead.

I have been following a tape which is meant to help you meet your guide. It is the second such tape that I have listened to. I have listened to them for several years now. I am coming to the conclusion, that whilst I may be doing the tapes, my guide is not.

Good news on the fish front. The angel fish have had babies! I had to drive to the shop to buy a plastic divider for the tank and special baby fish food. That was nearly twelve pounds gone. "I don't know why we do it really" I said to the man in the shop. I had to divide the father off from the mother as she kept beating him up. I guess that happens to a lot of fathers. It is strange isn't it, how animals and humans have such a wide range of reactions to the whole process of procreation.

Some love their partners and children, others see them only as a source of food. Some take the greatest care of their partners and offspring, others would destroy them without a moment's thought.

I have had time for two moon meditations recently. In one, I saw a large violet anemone with tentacles that reached out into space. In the second, also violet, I had a vivid impression of an enormous rounded lump of rock, its face covered with rounded craters, which was moving through space.

Sometimes, I think that we should not try to analyse these images too closely.

 eptember 14th,
Monday

There has been a total disaster on the baby angel fish front. The holes in the expensive dividing screen turned out to be just that little bit bigger than the baby fish. Whilst we ate our evening meal, the baby angel fish, filled with that indescribable suicidal joy of the very young, all wriggled through the holes to the other side of the tank. By the time I noticed, only 3 were left. The tank light also broke down, flashing on and off, just enough to ruin one's night vision. It was by now late at night. I caught the survivors by the light of a torch and put them in a floating tank called a trap which I had bought specially to hold baby fish.

We had had a roast dinner. (My guilt at eating meat having been replaced by guilt at not eating it because my body just does not seem to want to be vegetarian and the iron tablets are really upsetting my insides.) Jon unfortunately poured the fat down the sink, which blocked totally. We crawled off to bed and left it. Jon fixed it the next day.

The next morning, I discovered that the holes in the trap were also bigger than the baby fish and they had all escaped and been eaten.

In the small aquarium, the female platy that I bought recently died. She had babies first. I suspect her death was due to the exhaustion of motherhood.

In the bathroom, the bottom of the linen basket rotted off due to the constantly soaked floor.

Tara was due to have a birthday party in two weeks, but I just discovered that we are working then, so it will have to be this weekend at short notice.

Tara is taking recorder and violin lessons this term. I have to get her a violin and a recorder, plus a book. The school have also started the new government scheme where teachers have so much to do in the classroom that it is no longer possible for them to have time to teach the children. Thus, Tara has come home with tables and spellings to learn, in addition to the usual reading and for the weekend brought home a huge book to read which she was then meant to write about. Although it wrecked the weekend, we were unable to complete the work.

The work from the business that I have been unable to complete for the last six weeks of the summer holiday sits in heaps or sprawls over our dining table in drifts.

And the bathroom is full of spiders.

I admit it. I cannot cope. Things do not fit. There is no space, no time, no order. There is chaos. The depths of space are more ordered. (And certainly have more space.)

I cannot cope. O.K. Universe. All right! I surrender!

Some things have to change.

BANG!!!!!!!

There was a bang and a young pigeon just flew into the window of this room. It sat and looked at me for a few moments, seemingly unharmed and flew away. (And that is honestly true.)

September 24th, Thursday

We survived the children's party. No one fell in the pond, but it was very close with one. (His mother had phoned a few days before, worried about our pond.) There was a certain amount of shouting, but nothing was broken or damaged. To celebrate this fact, after they had all gone, Tara did some painting and got paint on our settee, table, her clothes and herself.

We are thinking of planning a food colouring free party next year and getting some extra help!

We have ordered waterproof flooring for the kitchen and bathroom and thrown out the rotten linen basket. Jon found wonderful wheeled plastic trolleys with drawers in a sale and these now live in the bathroom and Tara and Tawny's rooms.

We plan to move the rooms around, so I have a bigger office, Tara has Tawny's bedroom and Tawny has a room for herself. We hope to prevent the odd mixes of room use that have been causing chaos.

The cycle of life and death continues with the fish. The angel fish have laid more eggs and the rest of the fish are crowded in one part of the tank. The clown loaches that I bought to keep each other company are fighting. Death stalks the platys and neons in the other small tank. The pump that I had used to filter the water has started to burn out, filling the room with the smell of burnt rubber. Jon changed the water in the big aquarium today as I just cannot keep lifting gallons of water.

Jon's computer has broken down and will cost almost the cost of a new computer to mend. The answering machine has also broken.

Running up the down escalator through glue comes to mind.

I have terrible toothache. Two of our authors who are healers have suggested or sent help for the pain but both say I need a dentist. The dentist took X-rays but cannot tell which tooth is causing the pain.

The good part is that when I went to the dentist, Jon looked after Tawny and I went shopping alone. Bliss! I bought a skirt that was smart. I am tired of looking like a cross between an ageing hippy and Bagpuss.

I also bought a book of meditations for busy women. Will I find the time to read it? I borrowed a library book of meditations for busy people, but returned it unread. I also had books on relaxation and stress management, but returned them unread too. My pile of self improvement books was over one foot high and unread and clutter is of course, bad Feng Shui. (I am never sure how to pronounce it. I'll have a number 37 with prawn crackers please.)

I was following Feng Shui for a while. I asked Jon to remove all his knives from over the stairs as they were bad, (like the sword of Damocles) and now I feel that I should not have done this as they now live in a heap. Also, there were so many pins holding them up that the stairwell now seems to have been attacked by giant woodworm. The ideas about clutter seemed fine, but as you continue, each type of Feng Shui disagrees. It seems that we lack helpful people because we have the North West part of our house missing. Then I find that there seems to be almost no place that it is good to have a toilet. Eventually, like so many, I collapse into a confused heap.

I showed my Mum our bedroom. She screamed. Then she laughed. She said words like "Painful" and said, "It used to be such a nice room". We have painted parts of it a solid plum colour. It looks better. I am wondering about moving. Maybe I can call in the television "House Doctor" who will tell us how to decorate the house in order to sell it and undo what we have done following the ideas in "Changing Rooms".

Now I wonder what the clothes programmes will do to my dress sense?

Oh, by the way, some good news, either my bathroom scales have gone wrong, or I keep placing them on the wonky floor board, (I once "lost" one and a half stone that way) or I have lost half a stone in weight! Actually, the toothache helped! Also Jon, helping me eat less fattening meals. So far, he has avoided the problem of many husbands who have wives who want to lose weight and has not become thin himself!

 eptember 30th,
Wednesday

The bathroom is full of spiders again. I counted fifteen, despite Jon's continued vacuuming.

We were supposed to go caravanning in the New Forest, but it seems my Higher Self decided we should not go. It seemed a good idea, going with a group of Pagans that we know at the local pub moot, but it was not to be. Tara was looking forward to riding ponies and swimming. We had thought that we would have our own caravan, but many people that we had not met were due to come too and it seems we were to share with a family we did not know. It increasingly appeared that we were not meant to go.

Whatever the reason, things broke down and we all became ill. On the day of packing, the pump broke down in the small aquarium. Something had obviously been wrong for some time. Then water began to leak out of the tank. At first, at the back at the top, then sides and then, in the evening, all along the base. We phoned the shop and I was impressed as they said bring it back and we will replace it, no quibble about receipts or anything.

We finally decided not to go away and spent the evening rescuing the fish. Then we were all ill for the weekend. And it rained and rained and rained. We would have been drowned rats in a tin can had we been in a caravan.

The new aquarium is lovely and works far better than the last, which had also had the glass scratched and chipped by

Tawny banging it with a large quartz crystal. Perhaps she was trying to heal the fish?

We spent the weekend moving rooms. Jon did most of the moving as I cannot lift heavy things and he seems to like doing it. Anyway, he would not tell me his plans, so we kept crossing aims and trying to use the same space and he kept growling. I decided it was better to keep people fed. By the end of the weekend, he had painted half of Tara's new bedroom, turning it from my previous choice of spiritual violet to deep blue and moved the contents of nearly half the house. He did not feel well, so he was taking it easy.

Tara loves her new room in the roof which is huge and mysterious with sloping walls and low beams. Tawny loves her room downstairs with her toys easily to hand and where she can sleep hearing us all nearby in the day and early evening. I love the bigger office that I now have, with the new aquarium full of happier, healthier fish. It seems that my Higher Self must have listened when I suggested that it could help guide me in the right direction, not just by wrecking things, but by positive reinforcement too!

We have decided to paint over the werewolf-in-a-slaughter-house effect in our own bedroom with pale blue. It should take many coats! I think that the paint pattern is very eloquent and if we were to fit chunks of our ceiling into frames and sell them in a gallery with names like "Frantic" and "Desperate Frustration" we could sell them for hundreds of pounds.

It seems that there is a great need for blue at the moment. Traditionally a cold colour, rooms all over the country and even gardens are turning blue. We are thinking of painting the bathroom blue too. The problem is that as you start to change one room dramatically in a house, the others start to feel wrong.In the same way, certain "accepted" sacred sites are changing in their energies too. People may still meet there and have themselves photographed against the correct background of stones, but the positive energy does not feel there in the same way. It does not seem to be allowing itself to be used so freely and that which is positive is moving away from them.

Perhaps certain of these energies are moving to less well known places? Possibly, they are gradually changing to another level altogether?

Certainly, Avebury has changed over the last year. The stones of the Cove were fenced off because they were leaning. Even more than most things, what was happening there energy wise was far more than leaning stones. The fencing was no problem to them though. I felt that they liked it. I could feel the energy even more strongly from outside the fence. The Great Barn, which contained lovely people and infor-mation and sold local crafts in addition to our books was shut by the National Trust to make way for a virtual reality centre of all things! The Barn has sat there, a pointless, empty black hole all this year.

The Pagan gatherings at Avebury do not seem the same to me either. It is not simply the difference of opinion between those meeting there, some claiming the patch as theirs, (!) but that after standing for hours in the cold at the Winter Solstice, as people drifted away frozen and drained, forced to leave before the circle was closed, (which in itself leaves open all manner of energy drains unless one knows what is going on) some-thing in me changed. It seemed sad and as if energy was leaking away without point.

There are places which are peaceful and energising and many of them are not the "Great" and accepted sites. Possibly those who are sensitive will notice that they are actually moving and turning up in the strangest places! You do not need a stone circle or a photographer for a place to be magical!

ctober 8th, Thursday

We counted 20 spiders in the bathroom last night, despite vacuuming.

We also have mice in the garage, I have found several in the chicken food bin. I have tried telling them off before I let them go, but it does not seem to be working. It sounded like one running around our bedroom last night. I have set a live trap on the landing. One year they filled our roof and the cavity walls, coming up in the kitchen cupboards to create havoc. Even having a cat does not seem a good idea. We had one that used to catch them and release them live in the house. Then I had to catch them!

When I arrived at Tesco's on Friday, there were fire engines outside. I thought it was going to be quite interesting, but if the place had been on fire, people seemed unconcerned and to be being very British about it all. It turned out that they were just giving out leaflets.

It appeared to be costume day because the nuns were also shopping. I considered telling one that I used to be a nun in a past life but decided just to smile instead.

At the weekend we went to a Pagan conference. We arrived well after the start and were a little disconcerted to find only ten cars and a motorcycle in the car park. We thought that we had the wrong venue or the wrong day, but it

was right. There were only about thirty people there. As it was, they were very positive people and bought quite a few of our books.

One lady performed two ritual dances in the veiled belly dancing style. Tara said, "I can see her knickers!"

I phoned the organisers of the New Forest weekend and asked how it went. (It had rained heavily all weekend.) It went "quite well" it seems, people sat and chatted and drank quite a lot, he said, and he and his wife are giving up all their posts 'of responsibility and giving up organising things in future. I congratulated them.

It is interesting how many of the dependable and reliable people who could always be counted on to organise things for the rest of us are growing tired of being tired and too busy to have a life of their own and are refusing to do it any more.

We spent many years running a re-enactment society where people became less and less active and helpful until in the end, they proved themselves to be something very far from friends. Then we stopped doing it. We frequently meet others who have followed the same path.

Tawny is getting the hang of toddler-hood well. On one day this week, she scribbled all over the cheques that we had written and then found a jar of quince jelly and spilled it on the lounge and dining room carpets.

I am glad that we did not go to the Bahamas for a holiday this year. Chris Thomas suggested that it would be a very bad place to be later this season and the current hurricanes and travellers' tales of woe certainly bear that out.

ctobeʀ 12th, Monday

I am going to write about an incident last week. I was not going to originally, because it was so awful that it did not seem to have a place in amongst funny writing. I hope however, that amongst these words clear truths are revealing themselves to you.

Jon is diabetic. His health care has been far less than wonderful and he nearly died two years ago. Despite repeated requests for help our local surgery refused him access to the specialists that he needed and carried on until he collapsed and nearly died. He eventually reached hospital, where we were told that it was an absolute miracle that he remained alive to get there and a miracle that he had survived for years on the totally inadequate prescription of insulin that he had been given.

Even after his near death, the consultant care that the hospital said he would be placed under was not given. We went to a private doctor eventually. Her conclusions were extremely worrying and she told me to go to the surgery and talk to them. I was unhappy as their only recourse had been to batter me with repeated bullying attempts to break up our marriage and abandon Jon.

At no point would they discuss his health with me in a positive way, even if we went together. Even with us both there, the doctor refused to discuss his health and kept telling me to divorce him. I had been reduced to tears and shaking by such attacks in the past.

The private doctor told me to be positive and non emotional and that things might have changed.

I went to our surgery on Wednesday October 7th. I told the G.P. the private doctor's findings. She then, suggested that the one we had seen was not a doctor, and that Jon had not been attending his appointments, (not true since his change by the hospital to sensible insulin.) Several people have said that they would not blame him for avoiding people like those at our local practice anyway!

I was then urged to divorce him and go into a rescue centre, which it seems the wife of another of their diabetic patients has done, (I presume she received the same treatment that I have.)

Then she said, "...Let Nature take its course" "..he'll end up dead in a ditch somewhere" and that will "...resolve the problem". I still feel quite shocked. That is a gross understatement. I think that I went into shock for a couple of days. Then I started to talk to people.

I have talked to a counsellor from the British Diabetic Association, a psychologist, a counsellor, a homeopath and a spiritual healer, my Mum and some of our neighbours.

This practice however, has built a large new surgery, extended it and bought expensive computers and bought their staff uniforms! They have just closed one of their two surgeries, (they cover a vast area) and one doctor has put a letter in the local paper explaining how this will lead to a better service for their patients. (I bet the people in the village with no sensible bus service who are losing their surgery do not think so!)

"Something is rotten in the state of Denmark", as one of our authors would say.

# ctober 20th, Tuesday

I keep seeing shopping nuns. At least they appear to be buying better food for themselves than they were. I feel concerned about them. Even when I went into town, they were there with shopping bags. Are my Higher Self and my guides playing games with me on this?

I am also seeing dwarves. Maybe I had a previous life as a short person. Perhaps it is just that there is a big fair in town at the moment.

After my conversation with the doctor, we are considering moving. I am sure the doctors would be delighted to lose an "expensive family". Many things are meeting together to tell us that it might be time to go. Neighbours tell us that they are suffering terrible vandalism and theft, though it seems, (touch wood) that we have been protected for a while. Car chases pour into the village off the motorway. One was rolled in the road a few hundred yards from our house.

We are looking at Devon, where many small farmers are giving up and selling out. If we sell this house well, we could buy a wonderful place down there for the same money. We are also told there is high unemployment, so perhaps we could find people to help us with the business and child-care. I think about extra space, surfing, wonderful countryside, planting a wood and some people to work with us and help!

Mind you, we have to plan carefully. Anywhere we buy has to be high enough above sea level to avoid the dramatic rises in sea level that are due soon.

I had to visit the dentist in town. I walked into part of town, the edge of which was marked by a very short, square man. All the people behind him on the pavement were of an unpleasant and avoidable kind. The whole area that they filled had a strange kind of unpleasant energy and I was glad to enter a record shop and leave that piece of pavement.

Whilst in town, I bought myself a black cardigan with an enormous fluffy collar. I am told that ex-nuns have a tendency to wear black. I do not normally wear this colour, but the cardigan and that comment caused a reaction. This set off a clothing crisis, where I could not decide what to wear. Every time that I wore it, Jon referred to it as as my "Gorilla outfit" which eventually brought on another sort of crisis.

I have managed to shut up the chicken food bin so that the mouse could not get in. When I heard an odd noise from the compost bin outside the back door, guess who was there when I opened the lid?

The local paper carried an article on the huge number of spiders around this year. Tesco's have run out of insect and moth controls. Jon keeps vacuuming.

# ctobeR 26th, Monday

It has been a bad time for rodents. We were due to go away this weekend and had decided to leave the chickens with enough food for two days, thereby not having to try and find a neighbour to feed them. Then I realised that we had rats. This meant that the rats would steal all the food the first night and leave the chickens without food.

I called the "Environmental Services Department" (The Rat Man) and he came the next day. It seems it is a bad year for rodents and insect pests. He put down poison. Sadly, one cannot ignore rats. I have tried, but they do not respond to psychic nudges to leave, not when there are all too physical bowls of chicken food around.

I must say that our rats are very healthy looking, even when dead. They have a coat of fur on them which would win pet shows.

When I returned from the weekend, I opened the lid of the outside compost bin, which Jon had emptied before we left and inside were two starved bodies, a mouse and a vole.

Then today, we had new floor laid in the kitchen and bathroom. One man claimed that there was a dead mouse in the back of the cooker. I thought he was teasing me until he produced the gruesome evidence. He banged it down on the top of the cooker, reminiscent of the Monty Python dead parrot sketch. It had electrocuted itself on the wiring.

I am now rather nervous about opening things and removing lids as small rodent bodies keep appearing and I have to bury them. It does not seem respectful to put them in the wheely bin. I did send one rat off to the dump inside a plastic tub for a coffin. Another I buried in the vegetable plot but Jon was so horrified that he said he would concrete over the whole vegetable plot unless I dug it up again. I had buried it very deep, so my back was in a bad state after I finished the exhumation. (Or should it be ex-ratration?)

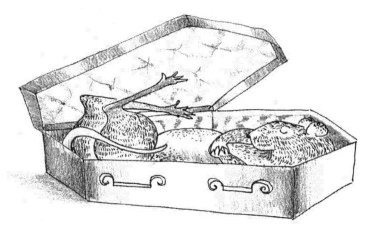

I tried to overdo things again at the weekend. We went to a Pagan conference to sell books and I gave a talk. We also went to stay with my Mum. In addition to that, I thought we could look at houses in Devon one day and drive down there on another to meet two of our authors. This was way over the top, especially as the weather and the traffic were a nightmare and the back fell off Jon's car's electronic wing-mirror and was lost. We did not reach Devon on either occasion.

Paddy Slade, another author and her son Bob were on the stall next to us at the show, selling his marvellous wood carvings.

I gave a talk on my first book, *Patchwork of Magic*. I had explained clearly that I would not give a talk as such, but have a discussion with the audience. The organisers ignored this totally and put me down as a talk anyway, which I discovered at 11.30 the night before.

It was an educational experience. No-one was there to introduce me. The vast majority of the other people there did not want to join in. I began to fear I was talking to tapioca pudding. Was I getting through? They laughed in places, but I was not able to do a solid hour of comedy which is what they seemed to expect.

In fact, I do not know what they were expecting as they would not answer my questions for the most part, but just sat there or left the room. People walked in and out throughout it.

About six people joined in and one lady spent several minutes relating a tale in full detail until I felt that I had definitely lost control though I was very grateful to those who spoke. I learned later that most of them were very new to Paganism and did not know where to start.

"What were you hoping to hear?" I asked them. "Would you like me to read from the book?" I did. After 45 minutes of the hour had gone, I handed over to a man there who wanted to talk about the eclipse in Cornwall, which gave him a spot.

Out of the talk, I spoke to several people individually about the changes that people and the world are going through and it felt good to hear others who are finding that their lives are altering in strange ways. I was able to give out ideas to help them understand parts of it all and hear their experiences which echoed, clarified and confirmed my own.

Tara was in workshops for children and Tawny stayed with my Mum for the day which gave me quite a break.

The Bristol Rag Morris danced at the end which was enjoyable and then, feeling tired, we decided not to stay for the evening party and we headed off to my Mum for the evening.

Having returned home on Sunday, today was chaos day. Jon kindly offered to work from home to support me. The washing machine repair man came really early and announced that all we had wrong was a blocked filter, which I should have checked and cleaned myself. (No housework points there!)

Then the two nice men also came and laid vinyl flooring in the kitchen and bathroom. It was one of them who found the electrocuted mouse mummy.

I had just put Tawny to sleep near the front door when a neighbour with a loud voice arrived selling poppies for Remembrance day. I told him about the two estate agents that we asked round to value the house last week. Their estimates varied by £50,000. He was not surprised and said that different agencies asked and received wildly different amounts on the same property.

We are calming down on looking at properties at present. I am told that if it is right it will flow, but I am not sure that moving house can ever flow.

# ctobeʀ 27th, Tuesday

It continues to rain and rain. The rain it raineth every day. And then some. I am expecting to see animals gathering in pairs soon. The West of the country has gales and rain and more rain and yet the East is dry.

I am trying to make the last of the straw last for the chickens as we cannot find a dry day for Jon to fetch more straw in an open trailer. The chicken runs are like bogs and the straw disappears.

Amazingly, our sunflowers are still standing, even our wonderful twelve foot giant. Tara is so proud of it.

I wondered if there was another side to all this weather and felt that it might have a cleansing effect, blowing out the cobwebs so to speak. Psychic grot or greyness can accumulate like a heavy dense blanket over an area, so perhaps this will wash it clean and blow it away.

There certainly seems to have been an air of fear around recently, especially after the local newspaper added to the latest list of local development plans the possibility of a toxic waste dump a few miles down the road in Newbury.

I am not sure that the vinyl floor in the kitchen and bathroom is totally the answer to my dreams. Mum had one fitted and it appears to have become wet underneath and has buckled. With the water that the children poured on the bathroom floor today, I am not sure how long ours will last.

There also seem to be gouge marks in the kitchen floor which we noticed soon after they left and we are not happy but do not feel like a confrontation. Why do so many things not quite go right?

It is half term this week, so the children are cooped up inside with the rainy weather. Tara and I went into the garden briefly today and yesterday we managed time in the park. Tawny is asleep now. Bliss!

ctobeR 30th, FRiday

When I looked in the kitchen cupboard, I discovered a cereal packet with a hole chewed in the corner. Next to it was a pile of raisins as the mouse did not appear to like raisins.

I set a live trap and caught a mouse at nearly midnight. I took it for a walk down the road and released it.

The next night, gone eleven at night, I caught a mouse, took it down the road and let it go. It looked suspiciously like the first mouse.

When I last caught mice, I eventually drove them for miles, letting them go well away from the house. If I had to wait a few hours before I released them, I fed them little titbits so

they did not starve. It was only after I started to drive them well away from the house that I stopped catching what may well have been the same few individuals!

At least the spiders seem reduced in numbers. Maybe the mice are eating them.

I phoned about the kitchen floor not being right and a nice man returned to look at our kitchen floor. He put in two new screws where two had come out and announced that the uneven marks were adhesive which should come out. He tried to rub it off himself, but unfortunately developed cramp in one leg and had to jump up and hop around exclaiming. (I eventually discovered that it was permanent damage, gouged into the surface, which is why I suppose he left so quickly.)

I felt brave to phone up. It takes a lot of nerve to do so, especially when there have been times when nearly everything that I have bought has proved faulty and I had to complain again and again. Perhaps it is character building?

In the past I have put great energy into helping another person and found everything in my life then went wrong. The person I was helping was certainly no friend of mine. They drained my life in every possible way and then tried to destroy what was left. Perhaps I am at last learning to listen when things begin to go awry.

It is so easy to see it in others, when they associate with those who damage them and cannot see that they need to pull away from such people. It has taken me many years, perhaps lifetimes to begin to learn to see it for myself at last.

We are conditioned to be far too nice. We are taught we should not complain or make a fuss and while we are busy being nice, we are walked over, cheated and abused. We are taught to look away politely and so learn not to notice the fangs that slip out through the lips of the wolf or vampire who are entering our lives.

I am learning at last that being nice, not looking and self sacrifice are terrible faults, which will not only result in suffering but are grossly unfair to one human being for the whole of their life, namely, the one who is busy being so nice and self sacrificing! Having said that, I suppose I should be really ruthless with the mice, but....

Regarding the continuing gales, I remembered that we often have such high winds a few weeks after America has had severe weather. This may thus be the weather that hit the Bahamas recently. If so, we are enjoying the Bahama weather without having to fly there!

November 2nd, Monday

I thought this morning that the three elderly bantams sat around their food bowl like the witches in Macbeth. It must have been a good rendition of the scene, as Jon came home for lunch and said that they looked like they were rehearsing for Macbeth.

And it is still raining, At least we have more straw in the garage again. I had felt deprived of water in this area, but currently feel glad not to live near a steadily rising river.

I have not caught any more mice for a few days, but on inspecting the trap, Jon told me that he had found a tiny note requesting bread, cheese and apple juice for breakfast and

asking me not to take the mouse out for his walk if it was raining.

It has been a very soggy Samhain or Hallowe'en. Those who choose to celebrate the changing of the seasons outside have my sympathy. We acknowledged the time with mead by a log fire in our lounge. We cut the apple in half sideways and there was revealed the star of hope. It was one of the largest and clearest that we have seen.

This was far better than a few years ago, when we cut the apple with "friends" present and there was no star! They later proved themselves to be quite something other than friends. I have ignored so many signs in my life and thought the best of the wrong people again and again. I hope that I have learned the right lessons.

On the Friday, Tara went to a children's fancy dress disco. She refused to go as a witch and went instead as a fairy, dressed in white. For Halloween itself, we waited with our pumpkin lantern and a cauldron full of sweets for the trick or treaters, or "cherry trees" as Tara called them, having misheard the words. The rain kept them away. Eventually, faced with our disappointment, Jon put some clothes out through a window and crept round to knock on the front door, dressed in a grey hooded cloak, a fur coat and with his face masked with a scarf.

After that, Tara and I had to do it, and when eventually two very wet trick or treaters reached us, we had eaten most of the chocolate. The children and I were dancing to music and we decided it was the best Halloween that we had ever had.

The next day we went to the Pagan moot at the pub. A regular visitor to the moot called John, who had given me reflexology massages before, did some dowsing work with me and came up with a collection of fascinating and helpful pieces of information. I asked which doctors at the surgery would be of benefit to our health and those who would not. I was surprised to be told that some doctors might care. Since John the dowser refused to let me tell him what had happened there recently beforehand, it was especially interesting that his conclusions with dowsing fitted with my experiences.

We also investigated several possible areas of geopathic stress in our house. (Basically, bad energy running through the Earth.) It seems that not only are we all sleeping in unhelpful areas, but the large aquarium is in a very bad position too. Interestingly, just before we went out, I found that the nitrates in that aquarium had shot sky high again and Jon did an emergency water change. John said that such energy grew worse when it was stormy and near the full moon.

Copper coils placed in the line of this bad energy should deflect it. I think that I should learn to dowse more myself too.

Our house painting continues. The hallway is now a glorious warm apricot. It looks great.

ovember 4th, Wednesday

There is a mouse running around the house. I used to be quite good at catching them when we had a cat who brought in live mice and let them go, but I think I am out of practice.

I have also tried both dowsing and a pendulum, though not as a means of rodent control. Asking questions appears to work well for a while but becomes nonsensical if I carry on too long and become tired. Jon made copper coils from old electric cable, stripping it down and winding it around a wooden spoon handle. I have placed two coils either side of the large aquarium to start with. It will be interesting to see what happens and if the constant troubles with this tank are improved.

Colour sketches of a cover illustration for my book, *Between Earth and Sky* arrived today. I really love the illustration!

Tawny now still a toddler, is developing Tara's love of painting. She likes to pretend to decorate, when we are painting. Yesterday, whilst I was painting our bedroom, I found her pretending with a sharp pair of scissors. I took them away and gave her a brush instead. Then, I looked away from the paint tin. When I looked back, she had very sensibly dipped her brush in and was painting the wall. Luckily, it was the right wall. I am still trying to cover all the burgundy in the bedroom. We keep thinking that we have finished, but like old blood stains, it keeps peeping through.

Tawny's other artistic creations include painting patterns in Soya milk, (she is allergic to dairy produce) on the front of the welsh dresser, and her floor decorating period. Jon used newspaper to cover the hall floor. She ran onto it until her feet were black and then imprinted these marks all over the new kitchen floor, which is mostly white. I tried to wipe these up and she then became black again and repeated it. Both children took it in turns to run into the kitchen and slip on the wet floor until it became wearing and no fun for any of us.

I am, as usual, reading several books at once. This is in addition to incoming manuscripts. I estimated that we have looked at over five hundred manuscript ideas and that does not include the early days for which I have no records.

I am currently reading about six books at once. One recently bought book is called, *"Meditations for Women Who do too Much"*. It contains short meditations for each day of the year about being a workaholic and ways to combat it. Sometimes I do not manage to read it. Other days, I read several days ahead.

I am also reading *"Women Who Run With the Wolves"* by Clarissa Pinkola Estes. It looks in detail at the deeper meanings in myths and traditional stories. Having read her version and explanation of "The Ugly Duckling" I feel that so many of us are swans who are living in farm yards full of ducks, or even worse, surrounded by flocks of vultures. Neither can help being what they are, but life is a great deal better when a swan finds the other swans.

I hope all the swans reading this are starting to recognise that they are swans and finding the other swans in their lives. I do hope that at long last, I am beginning to also.

ovember 12th, Thursday

Bonfire night was fun, both of them. We did not attend the firework display this year. It takes place just down the road from us. It was dark and cold and Tara is often frightened. Instead, we drew back the curtains in our lounge, turned the settee round, poured cider and mead and with sausages to eat, watched the display from our lounge.

At the weekend, we had a bonfire in the garden with sparklers. We burnt the linen basket and an old log basket. It was not quite the same as a wicker man, but more humane. Both evenings were great fun. Almost more so for not involving people other than our own small family.

The house is full of mice. I caught two more. The second mouse, I took for a drive. When I let it out, it was a baby, with big ears and huge eyes. It did not run away, but turned and looked at me. I really had to resist the temptation to take it back to its nice, warm home (our home) and its mother and look after it. Eventually, it settled down under a large toadstool. I had given it a piece of bread.

When I went there the next day, having worried about it during the night, the council verge cutting machine had come and the verge and toadstool had been trashed. I am now trying to deal with the guilt.

So many people are now noticing the speeding up in time that is occurring and also, so many feel tired. The only answer is to rest. There is great fear and anxiety too as the last vestiges of residual psychological and emotional baggage in many individuals continues to surface and be cleared.

I continue to see shopping nuns. Last week, it was another nun, in a different habit to all the other nuns. Soon, I will be seeing mice in habits. I am pleased to see that they still appear to be buying better food. (The nuns, not mice. The mice just steal ours, not being conditioned by years of guilt.)

If the nuns are also losing years of adverse conditioning and guilt is falling away from them as they do so, will I eventually see them clustered around the delicatesan or loaded down with lobsters? Already, I saw one buying far better, granary, multiseed bread, rather than the cheapest white sliced loaves they bought before. Where could it lead? As times continue to change, the priorities for where one might choose to live change. Not too near the sea and not near an Earthquake zone. Not too near a river and not in an area where the energies seem to worsen by the day.

Some people are living in their own little pools of golden light, others choose to move to a happier place. Those who are negative on the other hand, move to the negative places.

I tried using a pendulum and received many fascinating answers. The answers became stranger though. If we remained where we were, it said, everything we wanted would come to us, including the sea! We could also move house by taking the whole house! We have often said that is what we would like to do, (leaving behind the rodents, the spiders and the bindweed). That would be quite something, although the tricky part is connecting the services when you arrive at the other end.

It appears that part of the world is raising its vibrations to a more positive level. The other part is not. People must choose one side or the other. At the moment, it feels as if parts of me are vibrating at higher levels and parts at lower levels. All of us do this all the time, but I am feeling off balance and uncomfortably aware of it. This leaves me feeling very wobbly and rather faint. I feel like a bridge between the two. On occasions, a very rickety one.

As one part of the world rises in vibration and the other part lowers, life could become increasingly tricky. What if you vibrate at one level, but your house vibrates at another? You would be homeless! What if you sit down and your settee has changed vibration? You would fall straight through!

The thing is to hope that all the people that you really do not like vibrate at a different level to you. Hopefully, the things that you do like will stay with you!

Luckily, we are not in control of it anyway, so we may as well sit back and watch the fireworks! It is going to be one of the biggest shows that a planet has ever put on! Can I please have a packet of sparklers?

November 25th, Wednesday

Today is not the best of days. A vehicle has been backed into Jon's car, damaged it and driven off. The new fax machine, just bought due to the demise of the old one, refuses to work with our answerphone. After two days, Jon phoned the manufacturers to be told that it will only work with a special adaptor that they make and do not include with the machine. Thoughtful, that.

Tawny actually laid in this morning, but next door are having the house re-roofed. Amazingly, I was so exhausted that I slept over parts of the hammering. In the afternoon, the workmen became bored. To the words, "Disco Boys!" and "Party-time" one of them turned his car radio on really loud and treated the local environment, our chickens and my nerves to the result. I could not even play music to cover it as we had just had a power cut. New Age theory of light, love and fluffy bunnies states that one should not wish them a flat car battery. And definitely not that they fall off their scaffolding. Even a little bit.

Chris Thomas's comment to me the night before on the phone that part of the human race will be reincarnating on a planet thousands of light years away in future seemed wonderful. I am not sure if it is far enough away for certain people. They will probably have an entire culture based upon creating an amplifier big enough to annoy the heck out of that entire section of the universe.

There have probably been intergalactic protest meetings and people/aliens have tied themselves to asteroids and sat in front of multidimensional bulldozers to try to get them moved. When you think how many of the human race we do not want as neighbours, why should anyone or anything else?

At least the power is back on and I can now play an Irish music tape. It is a cheap tape and thus sounds as if it was recorded from inside a duvet, (or probably a tape recorder hidden inside a handbag at a concert) but at least it is my noise!

We went to the Pagan Federation main convention this weekend. We rose at 5.30 and scooped up the children. Driving up the motorway we saw one of the best sunrises I have ever seen. The last good one that I can remember was twenty years ago, rising and spreading through the sky over the cliffs and the sea at Weymouth.

Our stand did very well and it was great to catch up on all the news and gossip. I was a little confused as to why the closing rite was based on the rocky horror show and the druids were dressed in Gothic gear, but if I had attended the rite I am sure all would have been crystal clear.

A man came to our stand with spikes sticking through his nose and chin, which was rather weird. A lady was selling old fashioned corsets so during the day, some of the women went the most amazing shapes. We also met a lady who makes handmade shoes at a reasonable price and we are both thinking of having boots made. Shoe manufacturers think that our feet should fit their shoes. Well ours do not.

The painting which I commissioned for *Between Earth and Sky* was there. It is brilliant. It is our new catalogue cover. There is quite a strange feeling to have another person translate your visionary ideas into solid form in that way.

There are now thousands of copies of this painting and when my book is published, there will be thousands more. I bought the original.

I wore my new slinky green velvet dress. When I wore it to the Bristol conference it kept riding up at the back as it climbed my new black cardigan. I wore a different cardigan this time. Somehow though, my dress did not seem to fit properly. It seemed a strange shape with odd bulges and folds. At 1.15 the following morning, I discovered that all day I had been wearing my smart new dress back to front.

The next day was the school Christmas fair, quite a different event! Tara and I went to visit "Septic Mog". "She" appeared suspiciously to be male and had to wear various cloths around her head as she seemed to have a major facial hair problem. I was told information about myself which was quite accurate and sounded strangely like what I had been chatting about with one of the Mums outside the school recently. Interestingly enough, she was acting as "Septic Mog's" agent. Tara was told that there would soon be a family gathering with a tree covered in lights and there would be presents, which was, I must admit, very accurate, with Christmas coming and all.

Years ago, a lady borrowed props from me to be the Gypsy Fortune Teller at the hospital fete where my Mum worked. She was extremely accurate and was asked to repeat it the following year. She would not because her accuracy had frightened her too much.

ecember 3rd, Wednesday

The mouse war continues. It is getting out of hand. I am losing count of how many I have caught, or how many times I have caught the same one.

One in the lounge refuses to enter traps now and has become very tame. It comes out from under the settee when I am home alone and will come within a couple of feet of me. I nearly caught it underneath a bookcase and was lying on the floor facing it when it ran at me, striking the centre of my forehead hard. I screamed! I had the impression of a warm furry collision on my head for several hours.

We caught another in the live trap and I released it on the edge of woodland near an army base. They are very security conscious there, with the IRA and all and Tara said that a soldier was looking at me very intently when I let the mouse go. They have probably been on red alert for days since then.

I found a baby mouse trapped in a box in the office cupboard. it was very weak and despite my trying to feed it strawberry jam and water, (not having a minute intravenous glucose drip to hand) it died.) They have torn up a crisp packet in there and food is increasingly sealed in hard containers.

A mouse just ran across the floor of my office.

I bought another live trap as they seem too used to the other.   They cost four times as much as the deadly ones. In the shop I tried out a traditional trap, setting it and then trying to let it off with the sleeve of my coat. That did not work, so I tried again. sadly leaving my thumbnail too close to the trap and catching my thumb. Ow! Ow! I managed to keep quiet. I just hope no one in the shop saw me do it.

Jon suggested that I set up Mouse Aid and found an ageing rock star to record a charity song for them. I imagined myself sewing minute food sacks and dropping them off where I let them go. However, as they continue to devastate the house and seem to breed faster than I can catch them, I am increasingly less sympathetic to them. Possibly, I will have to do something drastic.

It is not just the stealing of food, but the mess and droppings. Also, they are very destructive. A previous invasion in the storage room in our roof led to many ruined things including a doll who had not only had her clothes and hair ravaged but had been torn limb from limb. My corn dolly did not come out of it well either.

Should we get a cat? Quite apart from the work, one previous favourite cat of ours would bring them in and let them go for us to catch! Jon would lock the cat flap and not let her in if he thought she had a mouse. She had to miaow to prove she was not carrying one. So she learned to miaow even when she did have a mouse! She dismembered one on our brand new, (at that time our only new) carpet. The stain is still there.

I used to be clever at catching them, but I think she had slowed them down for me first in the way that mother cats will for their kittens.

ecember 14th, Monday

"Against stupidity no herb has grown"

The previous quotation comes from another author, Lisa Sand and is originally German. I have just passed through a phase of people being exasperating. It is Dr. Lisa Sand who suggested that I was a nun in a previous life. She is a psychiatrist who works with those who are suffering trauma from previous lives. The conditioning from lives as monks or nuns is especially difficult to break in later incarnations. She has found that the laws of Chastity, Poverty and Obedience can be seared into the soul.

Herbal remedies that I have used recently have worked well, better than I remember before. My trips to the doctor this year have been about prescribed drugs and supplements which disagreed with me.

I am increasingly using herbal teas to help problems. Peppermint helps indigestion and I am trying camomile and other soothing drinks to try to relax more! When Tawny had sore red marks on her face, I considered the doctors, but then reconsidered. I made a cream using almond oil and lavender essential oil and the marks went very quickly. Since then, I have used my healing cream on sore places for myself and

Tara too. With the children, one dab is often enough for the soreness and redness to go.

Both Lisa and Chris agreed that natural remedies were increasingly working better. Chris believes that invasive chemical answers are becoming less and less effective. Often with harmful side effects, they suppress symptoms rather then healing the deeper causes.

We have not caught or seen any mice for several days. I had reached the end of my tether and begun to project images of fierce lethal mouse traps, poison and even getting a cat again. Perhaps this has telepathically been broadcast through the local rodent population?

Maybe it is just the change in the weather which has turned mild again. Which means, we are now back to rain, rain, rain.

I do wonder about getting a cat, but then I remember our previous cat who used to bring mice in to the house and let them go alive! The work of caring for an animal can be so great and the heartache is terrible if it all goes wrong. Our last cat became blind and deaf and died from cancer. She also had a terrible flea problem that drops from the vet and spraying the house repeatedly with awful organo phosphate derived insect sprays did not cure. Who clears up when the cat is sick? Mum of course. Who has to take her to the vet to be put to sleep? I do not feel that I could face all that again.

We have taken many family walks in the woods recently and I have talked to others who are increasingly withdrawing from the hurly-burly of the world where possible and enjoying Nature in simple ways.

We have great fun, swinging on rope swings, bouncing on a massive springy branch and Tara and Jon play with her big scooter. One day, Tara leapt from a steep high bank clutching the rope of a swing. She held it too low and landed in the soft squishy mud full of autumn leaves. She was dragged through this and then just sat there still holding the rope. I started to laugh. I could not stop. Even the fact that she was wearing her new school coat and her new trousers and I would have to try to clean it all did not stop me. I was sympathetic to her slightly bumped knee, but something in me just burst forth. Incredibly, it all washed off.

After a visit to the wood we carry wood home and make a log fire to toast crumpets and muffins on. We cannot use that week's wood as it is soaked, but the log pile is growing.

Everyone takes turns to toast and sometimes burn things. I give Tawny pieces of bread which she happily drops in the fire while we cook her muffins and crumpets for her. I have just bought two more toasting forks, so Jon will not have to tie a fork to the poker again.

The fire place really does become the heart of the home when we do this. When we had it built, I asked the builders to put in a bar so I could hang a cooking pot over it, but they could not cope with the idea. One builder had a house where there is not even a conventional oven, just a microwave to heat things up. In Wales, it is quite common for swivelling hooks called cranes to be fitted to fire places even now. We have often boiled a kettle on our open fire, until the warnings about aluminium put us off the kettle. We must buy a new non-aluminium one.

Perhaps, if certain predictions are right, we will all return to using such ancient methods to cook. Personally, I prefer them as a romantic extra!

December 21st, Monday

We went to visit Father Christmas and he gave Tara a pencil and ruler set and Tawny had a tape of "Favourite Christmas Songs". Except that the Twelve Days of Christmas is the only one that I have heard before. I came downstairs the next morning to hear the tape playing. Tawny was wagging her head back in time to the music, a golden cherubic smile on her face. Jon was not. Jon was muttering about tying two pillows to his head. He was saying that it would be worth paying two pounds to go back and 'see' Father Christmas and "I'm going to kill Father Christmas". Perhaps "Snowy the Snowman" sung in a happy cheerful manner, several times, had not been his ideal choice of music to start the day.

We have finally bought ourselves a video camera. This was at last spurred on because Tara was "Sound Effect One" for her school play. She stood, dressed in a wonderful snowflake costume which I had sewn part of, wearing the snowflake crown that we had made with her at home, beside the stage for the whole play, but was positioned in too dark a corner to come out on the official school video. We had bought a copy of this, thinking she would be on it, so it was doubly disappointing.

A trip to the woods was accompanied by the new camera. Tara and Jon and I all swung on ropes, bounced on branches and Jon and Tara flew down slopes on the scooter, but film as we might, no one fell over in a funny way. There was a close shave where Tara swung out a piece of wood on a rope and narrowly avoided being hit with it, but we are not sure if it would be quite funny enough to send to that video programme where you can earn large sums of money for pushing granny in the swimming pool and filming it. Tara did fall over and was left hanging by her coat as she slid down a steep slope, but she did it on the reverse side of a slope where we could not see her and so was not filmed. She was unhurt luckily, but muddy.

Tara has proved to be a right ham, inventing lines and "projecting" them in an excruciating manner.

When we returned home, we filmed us cooking crumpets. Tawny was allowed her own. She ate hers mostly raw and covered in ash. I believe charcoal is good for the digestion?

I filmed Tara putting decorations on the tree to the sound of Christmas carols from the television. She walked across the room and promptly turned the music off. At the next attempt, Tawny fetched a stool, rammed it into my foot and leg as I filmed, climbed up, looked into the lens and grabbed the camera. We have filmed less than fifteen minutes and we may have at least two pieces which might be worth sending in to the television programme already.

There are still no mice apparent in the house, though the damage they have caused is still coming to light. A bird-shaped tree decoration made from dough by Tawny at nursery had its head chewed off when we brought down the Christmas boxes. I was sad as I had looked forward to that appearing for many years.

The pest situation seems more positive nowadays. Jon was sitting at the table this morning when a gigantic spider walked across the table and into a plastic container on the table. Jon was able to scoop it up and remove it quite easily.

Our lounge and dining room are full of Christmas cards. We are especially lucky as the artists who have created wonderful images for our books tend to send brilliant cards. One of our authors sent us a photographic image of a famous stone with two rounded lobes. I presume its similarity to a gigantic bottom was an accident?

We are further ahead on our Christmas packing than before. Jon and I packed much together in front the fire when the children were in bed and it was fun. Today though, I packed his presents with Tawny and Tara helping and it was not relaxing! They both kept asking for sellotape. Tawny stuck hers on anything and Tara's present fell out of her package. We got there in the end. This year, we have bought a fair few items of chocolate. We can then give them to each other, removing them from the kitchen cupboard, wrapping them, taking them to my Mum's house, unwrapping them and bringing them back here to return to the kitchen cupboard. Logical?

My brother is a Major in the army. He is away for Christmas. This is not because of the Gulf War, (he was in the first,) but because he is sailing around South America for several weeks. They have drug smugglers, hurricanes, sharks and earthquakes. I am not sure that it would be safer to go to war. Last time he went, I said, "Never mind the enemy, watch out for the Americans." And I was right. They killed more of their own men and ours than the enemy.

I suppose that since this is meant to be a spiritual sort of diary, I should write wonderful spiritual things. Unfortunately, I have been far too busy preparing for the major religious festival of this country and have therefore had little time to be inspired.

Christmas Day, by the way, is a major time for women to have heart attacks.

# anuary 2nd 1999, Saturday

Yule was very quiet. We celebrated, as a family, with a venison stew and a log fire. We toasted the season with cider.

In the past, friends were invited to a Yule banquet, but so many proved themselves not to be friends, or at least drinking all the alcohol in the house that was meant to last the season, even proving to be total enemies and the custom has lapsed. There also used to be a Yule banquet in the re-enactment society which we ran for many years, but we have not been to that for over two years.

The postlady was given a box of chocolates for being so kind and trying not to wake me or Tawny early in the morning. If she guesses that Jon has just popped out to deliver Tara to school, she will sometimes drop the post in a little later when he has returned.

It truly is "Postman Pat" country out here. When a tree was delivered to us once, arriving after the Saturday post, one postman brought it to our house even though we were not due another delivery that weekend. Being a gardener himself, he did not want it to suffer over the weekend. We were out when he came. On returning, we were met by our cat, Grania, who was very vocal. Realising the poor telepathy of humans, she did her best to explain. "Miaow, miaow, miaow, miaow," she said. "Miaow!". Not wishing to leave the parcel on the front doorstep, the postman had gone to our back door and fed the narrow package in through our cat flap. Thus the vocal cat.

Christmas was quieter than usual, my Mum did not ask people in as in previous years, which made it less stressful and several of us commented on how much more enjoyable it was with fewer people involved. It appears that the more people are involved in anything, the more complicated and exhausting it becomes. We only stayed away a short time as the chickens were thus alright on their own with food and water.

My brother, who is currently in a ship's race sailing through the Panama canal, took the opportunity to "in absence" give Jon a tie for Christmas. It had pictures of ghosts and a cemetery on it and went 'Whoooo whoooo" when part of it was pressed. Jon said it might be useful for a funeral. There is an ancient tradition between them of Tim giving such presents which appears to have been restarted. In a previous year Jon was given a set of terracotta plant labels with the names of common garden weeds on them and a bath plug with a toy squeaking pig attached. Jon always showers.

Hopefully my brother will fare well. The recent Australian yacht tragedy where the race was hit by terrible weather is unsettling, as is the fact that before he joined the race his ship had the bilge pumps fitted the wrong way round so that they were pumping water into the ship instead of out of it.

For quite a time now, the "Doers" in life have removed themselves from positions of responsibility and barely disguised servitude to others. This does however mean that it can be very frustrating when you want help with anything! However, if you have been a "doer" for years, it can be true delight to begin to experience more time where things are done for your own pleasure!

Constantly, people are told to think of others and be selfless, until there is little of themselves left to hold them together. This year, we heard of several women who decided not to cook the traditional turkey dinner on Christmas day, but to enjoy it themselves. (Shock, horror!) How wonderful!

There are many viruses around at present and we, like so many others seem to suffer a round of sickness, diarrhoea, flu type feelings, aches, sore throats, colds, coughs etc. We keep burning essential oils such as lavender, eucalyptus and tee tree which fight viruses and support the immune system. Jon visited the shop at the local surgery which sells aromatherapy oils now and the lady there said that the essential oils appeared to be more successful than the cough medicines. If enough people bought Bach flower remedies, she would consider stocking them too.

We have been for many walks. Snelsmore, part of which now has the Newbury By-Pass built over it, has hard paths, so it seemed a good choice with all the rain. Unfortunately, they were not high enough above the surrounding area which had remembered that it is a peat bog and they were covered by large puddles and stretches of water. Tara greatly enjoyed scooting through them and we had to be very insistent that she did not enter the puddles off the path as there was no certainty of their depth. She became covered in water and mud up to the top of her legs and the school coat was in the wash again. Jon also discovered that his wellington boots leak.

Yesterday we walked in our favourite beech woods. Tawny fell in the mud right beside the car. Then when Tara was on the rope swing over the patch of wet goo and leaves that she had fallen into before, Tawny walked into the path of the swing. Jon tried to reach her, but was not able to stop Tawny being knocked into the wet mud. Unfortunately, we did not have the video camera with us.

The woods are increasingly filling with adults who play on the rope swings or ride bikes down the slopes. Jumps have been constructed and paths cleared through the leaves with a shovel The shovel was left leaning against a tree. Usually, it is quiet, but two of the adults were noisy. There is an air of increasing playfulness building in the woods.

Tonight we videoed Tawny eating a bowl full of home-made chocolate mousse. In the past, she has smeared this over her face and emptied the bowl on her head, but now we have the camera, she ate it with good manners.

Jon made the mousse with Tara this morning. Yesterday I made pizza dough with both children. They kept adding water and flour when I was not looking, so the mixtures increased in size. Tawny poured lemonade into hers and I rescued the cough mixture which she also tried to add. One end of the kitchen was covered in flour. I stayed calm and started to clear up. Unfortunately, they helped. Tawny sprinkled oil on the other end of the kitchen floor and I walked the oil and flour into each other before I realised what she had done. Luckily, Jon arrived at this point and removed the children so I could sort it all out. "At least you had not just cleaned the floor" he commented cheerfully from a safe distance. My Mary Poppins/Sound of Music personna was slipping. (Not surprising with the oil on the floor.)

Both children cut shapes from the dough with animal pastry cutters. Tara also made two strange thick lumps which she will not eat and which bang on a hard surface like rocks. Sometimes, even the chickens will not eat these. Our cockerel broke the end off his beak once (it regrew); I am suspicious as to the cause.

# anuary 22nd, Friday

Yesterday I saw the first snowdrops in our garden. This makes it Imbolc traditionally. Modern Pagans place it at the start of February, but I prefer to wait for the flowers that herald the first stirrings of Spring.

Years ago, at one of our Dark Age banquets, I explained Imbolc as best I could to those sitting at the table. I told them of the candles, the lights and of the goddess Bride. I also told them of the lactation of the ewes. In perplexed solemnity, one man then stood and toasted, "The lactation of the ewes" and everyone chorused the words!

My brother returned safely. The trip was not what he had expected and much of the time was spent fixing the problems with the boat. His boat beat the other forces' boats though, including the Navy!

My Mother, brother and his wife and twin babies all came to celebrate Tawny's birthday. It was a lovely day and the video was much in use.

Jon has been on television. This is not due to him talking about Paganism as he did on the local radio at Yule. He went into the Vodaphone offices to collect a leaflet on phones and they happened to be filming. They are trying to build an extensive headquarters on a field near Newbury. It is embarrassing to have been seen there, when so many locals are fighting against it!

Protesting came back to haunt us too, when the Newbury by-pass demonstration caused chaos one weekend. For the second time ever, I ran out of soya milk for Tawny and a quick trip to Tesco's took one and a half hours rather than a few minutes. We decided to head for home as fast as we were able in the traffic chaos, when we saw a policeman with a machine gun.

We objected to the destruction of so many trees for the by-pass and the use of nature reserves to build it on, but fail to understand what the chaos is meant to do now apart from make life a misery for the locals. Thank goodness we were not trying to reach a hospital.

Poppy Palin, another of our authors has carried out past life work for me. The results were stunningly accurate and have helped clarify many things. A key lifetime that she described was as a Celtic weaver. Interesting considering over twenty years spent in re-enactment societies as a Celt! I can feel the results of that pushing me forward into a new phase. So much of what she wrote is so accurate and reverberates throughout my current life situation.

At this time of year, it is often considered a time for making New Year resolutions. I have never liked these. They usually consist of a list of knuckle rapping accusations which result in a rapid feeling of failure.

I shall therefore simply resolve to enjoy life more.

It may also be a good time to look back at what has happened. Six months ago, I joked that I would write my diary in less than a year to beat all the others to press. I feel that now is a natural time to stop and consider what has taken place as it feels as if new energies are about to enter my life. (Again!)

What has happened in the past year? In all the madness and chaos, I have been changing. I have examined and faced several major issues and pieces of conditioning.

One was that of not harming anything. In the past, the house has filled with ants and even cat fleas (and yes, I did kill them as best I could.) In the last six months, it was spiders and mice. The spiders had to be vacuumed, which Jon dealt with, so the problem returned, this time with mice. It was not until my nerve had finally cracked and I had decided that it was them or me and started to project pictures of cats and lethal mouse traps that they chose to leave. I had also considerably reduced my guilt at breaking up their family groups and throwing them out in the cold. (Well - slightly less guilty)

My view of doctors and the traditional medicine has changed greatly. Already damaged by previous experience, it took a further nosedive this year. Herbal, Homeopathic, Bach Flower Remedies, Aromatherapy, all have found an increasing place in the health care in this house.

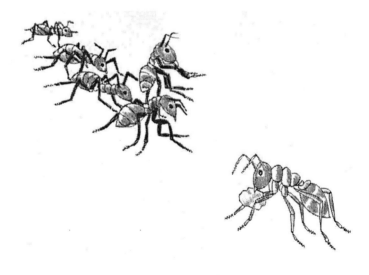

Another major set of conditioning was that of a monastic life. The nuns incidentally, are no longer appearing when I go shopping. The food that the nuns bought improved over the weeks, though I am not sure if this indicates that they are treating themselves better, or whether that too was a sign to me, that I was beginning to treat myself better, or both!

I worked through problems with clothing, the nun personality feeling that I should not look nice. I overcame my tendency to tear clothes or burn holes in them, reducing this to having them ride up at the back or wearing them back to front! Hopefully that too is a piece of conditioning now laid to rest.

I began to eat more meat. (Vegetarians miss this bit.) The situation was probably changing round about the time that I bought a vegetarian magazine at the start of my shopping trip and half way round was drooling over the steak. I even managed to eat a piece of steak this week which was not tough. My guilty side must be lessening its hold there. I would prefer not to eat animals, but have to admit that my body is healthier now than it was. I have spent a fortune on iron tablets that my body punishes me for terribly if I take them. At Christmas I gave my mother pots of mixed vitamins which I cannot use myself as they contain iron and she feels that we must be trying to build her up!

Increasingly it became possible to enjoy ourselves, even, (shock, horror!) to spend money on that enjoyment.

We spent more money on ourselves, (which the January credit card bill clearly demonstrates.) We bought things because we are worth it.

We learnt to play more, at first swimming and then playing in the woods. We laugh more.

I am learning to say "No" more too. That will take time and practice, but once started, it becomes easier each time as does life when it is not full of things that we do not want and which harm us and slow us down.

I am learning to let others wait for longer. I cannot go any faster. There are things which flow smoothly and those which do not. Increasingly, I will choose that which shows less resistance. Often, a change will occur which will then make the slow thing run smoothly again.

I am learning to speak my own mind more. Others may not thank me for it, but I no longer feel that I can hide hurt inside. Most of all, I have begun to lose a little of the massive load of guilt that I have felt myself to carry for lifetimes. I have begun to understand a few more of the lessons that I have been working upon.

I feel that I have moved forward and had fun in the process. We cannot ask much more of life than that.

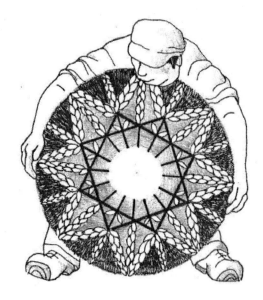

Snowdrop Song

Autumn leaves are lying on the ground.
The dead leaves are lying all around.

The snowdrops are peeping through the ground.
They are tiny, they are delicate,
But they are white and very very strong.

The snow is lying all around.
Its cold weight burdening the ground.

The snowdrops are peeping through the ground.
They are tiny, they are delicate,
But they are white and very very strong.

The ground is frozen all around.
Almost sleeping.

The snowdrops are peeping through the ground.
They are tiny, they are delicate,
But they are white and very very strong.

Spring is coming all around.
Spring is coming.
Spring is coming.

Imbolc

Tara, Jon, Tawny and I went to the woods and there we found a new spring rising at the foot of an alder tree.

We toasted the season with a hip flask of mead and celebrated with dark organic chocolate.

Bibliography

Armstrong, Karen, *Through the Narrow Gate - A Nun's Story*, Macmillan, 1981

Armstrong, Karen, *Beginning the World*, Macmillan, 1983

Hector, Terri, *A Breath Behind Time - Healing Through the Goddess and the Revealer*, Capall Bann, 1999

Palin, Poppy, *Season of Sorcery*, Capall Bann, 1998

Palin, Poppy, *Wildwitch - The Craft of the Natural Psychic*, Capall Bann, 1999

Palin, Poppy, *Soul Resurgence - A Guide to Reincarnation* (Capall Bann 2000)

Palin, Poppy, *Walking With Spirit, A Guide For the Natural Psychic* (Capall Bann 2000)

Pinkola Estes, Clarissa, *Women Who Run With the Wolves*, Random House, 1992

Russel, Mary, *Vortex, The End of History*, 1999

Sand, Lisa, *Medicine for the Coming Age*, Capall Bann, 1999

Thomas, Chris, *The Journey Home*, Capall Bann, 1998

Thomas, Chris, *The Fool's First Steps*, Capall Bann, 1999

Thomas, Chris and Baker, Diane, *The Healing Book*, Capall Bann, 1998

Thomas, Chris and Baker, Diane, *Everything You Always Wanted to Know About Your Body, But so far, Nobody's Been Able to Tell You*, Capall Bann, 1999

Wilson Schaef, *Meditations for Women Who Do Too Much*, Anne, Harper Collins, 1990

Also by Julia Day, published by Capall Bann:

Between Earth and Sky   by Julia Day

"If you want to know how to apply Paganism in daily life, then this is the book for you. Her Paganism is one of spontaneous joyful pragmatism..excellent and expressive" Wiccan Rede
"I thoroughly enjoyed it. I liked the poems, the musings and especially the workings. It was like talking to a friend over the phone. It is an easy read and holds gems of advice...a cracking book - like slippers, nice and comfy." Touchstone
"..a rich source of inspiration..this one is a gem" Michael Hoadley
Julia is a member of a Celtic Tradition. "I believe that whatever our beliefs or Tradition, we each make and follow our own path. I hope this book may help you to follow yours." *"Between Earth and Sky"* is a collection of articles, environmental reports, thoughts, visualisations, poems and stories, together with inspired writings which may help the reader to explore their own thoughts and feelings in many areas of magical, Pagan life."We are seeking to reconcile the physical world and spirit, the Earth and the Sky, just as we have always done. Earth below and Sky above. It is in that tension between the two that we learn and develop. As with the active and passive principle, the instrument of fertilisation and that which is made fertile, Male and Female, it is within that tension, that both the religion and our own development remains alive." *Patchwork of Magic.* ISBN 186163 0506   £9.95   Illustrated

Patchwork of Magic - Living In a Pagan World   by Julia Day

"Probably one of the most commonsense books I've ever read about Paganism" Michael Hoadley
"I believe your Patchwork of Magic should be read by all those who are about to start their journey" RC, Coventry
"....wise counsel based on personal experience...should be required reading. Highly recommended.“ The Cauldron.   *"...extremely funny...beautifully trashes the pretentious....clear and sane, totally grounded....rich in common sense."* OBOD Touchstone.   *"...packed with page after page of wonderfully witty and humourous material...written with common sense, a sense of fun and feeling ....you'll love it."* Time between Times
"this really is the 'Path of the Hearthfire' at its best...very down to earth...refreshing in its simplicity and honesty" The Wiccan Rede

A patchwork is composed of numerous coloured pieces, sewn together to make something beautiful and practical. This book contains many experiences, facts, thoughts and ideas. It has a light-hearted look at Pagan life and compares subdivisions which have formed within that world, groups as diverse as Druids and Chaos workers. Includes making incense, magic during everyday activities, initiation, help with personal development, grounding, centring, learning from dreams, recognising synchronicity and living an increasingly magical life. This book combines the natural energies of Earth and Sky, sewn together with love and laughter. ISBN 1898 307210   £9.95 190 pages Illustrated

FREE DETAILED CATALOGUE

Capall Bann is owned and run by people actively involved in many of the areas in which we publish. A detailed illustrated catalogue is available on request, SAE or International Postal Coupon appreciated. **Titles can be ordered direct from Capall Bann, post free in the UK** (cheque or PO with order) or from good bookshops and specialist outlets.

Do contact us for details on the latest releases at: **Capall Bann Publishing, Freshfields, Chieveley, Berks, RG20 8TF.** Titles include:

A Breath Behind Time, Terri Hector
Angels and Goddesses - Celtic Christianity & Paganism, M. Howard
Arthur - The Legend Unveiled, C Johnson & E Lung
Astrology The Inner Eye - A Guide in Everyday Language, E Smith
Auguries and Omens - The Magical Lore of Birds, Yvonne Aburrow
Asyniur - Womens Mysteries in the Northern Tradition, S McGrath
Beginnings - Geomancy, Builder's Rites & Electional Astrology in the
     European Tradition, Nigel Pennick
Between Earth and Sky, Julia Day
Book of the Veil , Peter Paddon
Caer Sidhe - Celtic Astrology and Astronomy, Vol 1, Michael Bayley
Caer Sidhe - Celtic Astrology and Astronomy, Vol 2 M Bayley
Call of the Horned Piper, Nigel Jackson
Cat's Company, Ann Walker
Celtic Faery Shamanism, Catrin James
Celtic Faery Shamanism - The Wisdom of the Otherworld, Catrin James
Celtic Lore & Druidic Ritual, Rhiannon Ryall
Celtic Sacrifice - Pre Christian Ritual & Religion, Marion Pearce
Celtic Saints and the Glastonbury Zodiac, Mary Caine
Circle and the Square, Jack Gale
Compleat Vampyre - The Vampyre Shaman, Nigel Jackson
Creating Form From the Mist - The Wisdom of Women in Celtic Myth and
     Culture, Lynne Sinclair-Wood
Crystal Clear - A Guide to Quartz Crystal, Jennifer Dent
Crystal Doorways, Simon & Sue Lilly
Crossing the Borderlines - Guising, Masking & Ritual Animal Disguise in the
     European Tradition, Nigel Pennick
Dragons of the West, Nigel Pennick
Earth Dance - A Year of Pagan Rituals, Jan Brodie
Earth Harmony - Places of Power, Holiness & Healing, Nigel Pennick

Earth Magic, Margaret McArthur
Eildon Tree (The) Romany Language & Lore, Michael Hoadley
Enchanted Forest - The Magical Lore of Trees, Yvonne Aburrow
Eternal Priestess, Sage Weston
Eternally Yours Faithfully, Roy Radford & Evelyn Gregory
Everything You Always Wanted To Know About Your Body, But So Far
    Nobody's Been Able To Tell You, Chris Thomas & D Baker
Face of the Deep - Healing Body & Soul, Penny Allen
Fairies in the Irish Tradition, Molly Gowen
Familiars - Animal Powers of Britain, Anna Franklin
Fool's First Steps, (The) Chris Thomas
Forest Paths - Tree Divination, Brian Harrison, Ill. S. Rouse
From Past to Future Life, Dr Roger Webber
Gardening For Wildlife Ron Wilson
God Year, The, Nigel Pennick & Helen Field
Goddess on the Cross, Dr George Young
Goddess Year, The, Nigel Pennick & Helen Field
Goddesses, Guardians & Groves, Jack Gale
Handbook For Pagan Healers, Liz Joan
Handbook of Fairies, Ronan Coghlan
Healing Book, The, Chris Thomas and Diane Baker
Healing Homes, Jennifer Dent
Healing Journeys, Paul Williamson
Healing Stones, Sue Philips
Herb Craft - Shamanic & Ritual Use of Herbs, Lavender & Franklin
Hidden Heritage - Exploring Ancient Essex, Terry Johnson
Hub of the Wheel, Skytoucher
In Search of Herne the Hunter, Eric Fitch
Inner Celtia, Alan Richardson & David Annwn
Inner Mysteries of the Goths, Nigel Pennick
Inner Space Workbook - Develop Thru Tarot, C Summers & J Vayne
Intuitive Journey, Ann Walker Isis - African Queen, Akkadia Ford
Journey Home, The, Chris Thomas
Kecks, Keddles & Kesh - Celtic Lang & The Cog Almanac, Bayley
Language of the Psycards, Berenice
Legend of Robin Hood, The, Richard Rutherford-Moore
Lid Off the Cauldron, Patricia Crowther
Light From the Shadows - Modern Traditional Witchcraft, Gwyn
Living Tarot, Ann Walker
Lore of the Sacred Horse, Marion Davies
Lost Lands & Sunken Cities (2nd ed.), Nigel Pennick
Magic of Herbs - A Complete Home Herbal, Rhiannon Ryall
Magical Guardians - Exploring the Spirit and Nature of Trees, Philip Heselton
Magical History of the Horse, Janet Farrar & Virginia Russell
Magical Lore of Animals, Yvonne Aburrow
Magical Lore of Cats, Marion Davies

114

Magical Lore of Herbs, Marion Davies
Magick Without Peers, Ariadne Rainbird & David Rankine
Masks of Misrule - Horned God & His Cult in Europe, Nigel Jackson
Medicine For The Coming Age, Lisa Sand MD
Medium Rare - Reminiscences of a Clairvoyant, Muriel Renard
Menopausal Woman on the Run, Jaki da Costa
Mind Massage - 60 Creative Visualisations, Marlene Maundrill
Mirrors of Magic - Evoking the Spirit of the Dewponds, P Heselton
Moon Mysteries, Jan Brodie
Mysteries of the Runes, Michael Howard
Mystic Life of Animals, Ann Walker
New Celtic Oracle The, Nigel Pennick & Nigel Jackson
Oracle of Geomancy, Nigel Pennick
Pagan Feasts - Seasonal Food for the 8 Festivals, Franklin & Phillips
Patchwork of Magic - Living in a Pagan World, Julia Day
Pathworking - A Practical Book of Guided Meditations, Pete Jennings
Personal Power, Anna Franklin
Pickingill Papers - The Origins of Gardnerian Wicca, Bill Liddell
Pillars of Tubal Cain, Nigel Jackson
Places of Pilgrimage and Healing, Adrian Cooper
Practical Divining, Richard Foord
Practical Meditation, Steve Hounsome
Practical Spirituality, Steve Hounsome
Psychic Self Defence - Real Solutions, Jan Brodie
Real Fairies, David Tame
Reality - How It Works & Why It Mostly Doesn't, Rik Dent
Romany Tapestry, Michael Houghton
Runic Astrology, Nigel Pennick
Sacred Animals, Gordon MacLellan
Sacred Celtic Animals, Marion Davies, Ill. Simon Rouse
Sacred Dorset - On the Path of the Dragon, Peter Knight
Sacred Grove - The Mysteries of the Forest, Yvonne Aburrow
Sacred Geometry, Nigel Pennick
Sacred Nature, Ancient Wisdom & Modern Meanings, A Cooper
Sacred Ring - Pagan Origins of British Folk Festivals, M. Howard
Season of Sorcery - On Becoming a Wisewoman, Poppy Palin
Seasonal Magic - Diary of a Village Witch, Paddy Slade
Secret Places of the Goddess, Philip Heselton
Secret Signs & Sigils, Nigel Pennick
Self Enlightenment, Mayan O'Brien
Spirits of the Air, Jaq D Hawkins
Spirits of the Earth, Jaq D Hawkins
Spirits of the Earth, Jaq D Hawkins
Stony Gaze, Investigating Celtic Heads John Billingsley
Stumbling Through the Undergrowth , Mark Kirwan-Heyhoe
Subterranean Kingdom, The, revised 2nd ed, Nigel Pennick

Symbols of Ancient Gods, Rhiannon Ryall
Talking to the Earth, Gordon MacLellan
Taming the Wolf - Full Moon Meditations, Steve Hounsome
Teachings of the Wisewomen, Rhiannon Ryall
The Other Kingdoms Speak, Helena Hawley
Tree: Essence of Healing, Simon & Sue Lilly
Tree: Essence, Spirit & Teacher, Simon & Sue Lilly
Through the Veil, Peter Paddon
Torch and the Spear, Patrick Regan
Understanding Chaos Magic, Jaq D Hawkins
Vortex - The End of History, Mary Russell
Warp and Weft - In Search of the I-Ching, William de Fancourt
Warriors at the Edge of Time, Jan Fry
Water Witches, Tony Steele
Way of the Magus, Michael Howard
Weaving a Web of Magic, Rhiannon Ryall
West Country Wicca, Rhiannon Ryall
Wildwitch - The Craft of the Natural Psychic, Poppy Palin
Wildwood King , Philip Kane
Witches of Oz, Matthew & Julia Philips
Wondrous Land - The Faery Faith of Ireland by Dr Kay Mullin
Working With the Merlin, Geoff Hughes
Your Talking Pet, Ann Walker

FREE detailed catalogue and FREE 'Inspiration' magazine
Contact: Capall Bann Publishing, Freshfields, Chieveley, Berks, RG20 8TF